Preservation of the Integrity of Electronic Records

D0031909

THE ARCHIVIST'S LIBRARY

Volume 2

Preservation of the Integrity of Electronic Records

by

Luciana Duranti
*University of British Columbia,
Vancouver, U.S.A.*

Terry Eastwood
*University of British Columbia,
Vancouver, U.S.A.*

Heather MacNeil
*University of British Columbia,
Vancouver, U.S.A.*

KLUWER ACADEMIC PUBLISHERS
DORDRECHT / BOSTON / LONDON

A C.I.P. Catalogue record for this book is available from the Library of Congress.

ISBN 1-4020-0991-7

Published by Kluwer Academic Publishers,
P.O. Box 17, 3300 AA Dordrecht, The Netherlands.

Sold and distributed in North, Central and South America
by Kluwer Academic Publishers,
101 Philip Drive, Norwell, MA 02061, U.S.A.

In all other countries, sold and distributed
by Kluwer Academic Publishers,
P.O. Box 322, 3300 AH Dordrecht, The Netherlands.

Printed on acid-free paper

Table of Contents

Acknowledgements

The research for this book was generously supported by a grant from the Social Sciences and Humanities Research Council of Canada. We were also assisted by representatives of a records management task force of the United States Department of Defense, whose role is acknowledged in the introduction to this book. We wish to acknowledge the assistance of Margaret Hedstrom and Rick Klumpenhouwer, who took part in research conducted in Sweden and the Netherlands. From time to time, colleagues contributed to discussion during research meetings. In particular, we wish to thank Maria Guercio, who became a regular participant in the research while a visiting professor, and Isa Poupard from Brazil, who lent us her expertise while a visiting scholar in our School. Charles Dollar, Glenda Acland from Australia, and Borje Justrell from Sweden also attended research meetings. We wish to thank the 3M Corporation, which hosted one of the research meetings in Minneapolis. We are grateful for the moral and intellectual support extended to us by colleagues and students in the School of Library, Archival and Information Studies at the University of British Columbia. Two students deserve special mention. Ian McAndrew assembled the various parts of the book, formatted them, and prepared a first draft of the scheme for the index, all with great care and devotion, for which we cannot thank him enough. Monica Greenan worked extensively in the final stages to insure that a long delayed book finally made its way to the publisher. She also prepared the subject index.

Introduction
By Terry Eastwood

This book reports the findings of a research project on the means of protecting the integrity of active and semi-active electronic records. The project, which is commonly referred to as "the UBC Project," was conceived by two of the authors of this book, Luciana Duranti and Terry Eastwood, and conducted between 1994 and 1997. The third author, Heather MacNeil, who worked formally as the principal research assistant on the project, acted as an equal in the research and in the writing of this book.

The project investigated a number of fundamental questions that have arisen over the past decade as a consequence of the rapid development and use of computer technology for the creation, maintenance, and preservation of recorded information. One of the first comprehensive studies of the issues associated with the management of electronic records was conducted by the United Nations. The study, commonly known as the ACCIS report, aimed to "develop guidelines for implementation of electronic archives and records management programmes for use by United Nations organizations, taking into account traditional archives and records management practices." The report of the study of electronic records in eighteen United Nations organizations identified a number of enduring issues. It recognized that the United Nations had to "distinguish between record and non-record material."[1] It recognized the problem of ensuring the authenticity of records, which, rather narrowly, it construed as "assuring legality." As the report put it, "the legality of electronic records will depend on evidence to show that creating records was normal operating procedure [which of course means that specific procedures must exist and be followed] and that appropriate care was exercised during the life cycle of the record to ensure continuity and inviolability of the record."[2]- It also recognized, somewhat obliquely, that recordkeeping capability had to be built into electronic systems.

> Because [electronic information] exists without anyone knowing it directly or being able to extract its meaning without an intermediary device, the designers of an electronic information system inevitably determine the kinds of records it creates. Also, because electronic records are at some point managed by an electronic information system, and because they are inseparable from that system except by means of facilities integral to the system itself, records managers must be involved in the design of those systems to ensure that the records passing through them serve organizational needs of accountability.[3]

In particular, the ACCIS report recommended that design had to "document" records, that is, ensure that they could be properly identified. It also recognized the need to institute procedural controls either inside or outside the system itself to control access to records, ensure the security of records from unauthorized change or deletion, and facilitate disposition, storage, and conversion or migration of records.[4]

Organizations all over the world were facing problems similar to those the ACCIS report found in United Nations organizations. Some observers reckoned that the problem could be traced to an almost complete lack of any of the normal rules governing creation and management of records in the new electronic environment. John McDonald, for example, writing in the mid-1990s, likened "the modern office" to "the wild frontier" where

> ... Office workers can create and send electronic messages and documents to whomever they wish. They can store them according to their own individual needs and then delete them without turning to anyone else for approval. There are no rules of the road. The autonomy of the individual reigns supreme!

He went on to argue that this situation was changing as organizations adopted "integrated software supporting directly the automation of work processes (designed to enhance organizational effectiveness.)"[5] At the time McDonald was writing, archivists had abundant evidence that document management systems and databases used to support office work did not meet recordkeeping requirements. However, as Margaret Hedstrom noted, archivists are not alone in recognizing the need to support business processes by developing "trusted systems" in areas related to electronic recordkeeping. She characterized such systems as "systems that can be relied on to follow certain rules at all times." She then went on to say:

> Record-keeping systems are a type of trusted system where rules govern which documents are eligible for inclusion in the record-keeping system, who may place records in the system and retrieve records from it, what may be done to and with a record, how long records remain in the system, and how records are removed from it... Such systems can be trusted only to the extent that the personnel who carry out record-keeping procedures know and follow record-keeping rules at all times... With the increasing use of computer-based information systems, contemporary organizations are seeking ways to replace [traditional] record-keeping systems which require that all participants in the record-generating process learn and follow rules for record-keeping with systems where the rules are imbedded in and enforced by software routines. In doing so organizations are seeking trusted record-keeping systems that follow rules for records creation, maintenance, and preservation at all times.[6]

In the world at large, the development of trusted systems is driven primarily by electronic commerce. Efforts to develop secure systems for electronic commerce and transmission of messages raise some of the issues important to the development of trusted recordkeeping systems, but they do not approach the problem from a comprehensive standpoint. What does it mean to have a trusted recordkeeping system such as Hedstrom generally outlines? What is the conceptual basis of the rules of which Hedstrom speaks?

Finding a solution to the problem is not simply a matter of finding ways to transplant recordkeeping requirements into the electronic environment. In the automated office, some documents are created simply to disseminate information, some are required for reference, some result from automatic recording of observations, and others are the product of actions and decisions of organizations. Not all data, information, and documents are records, but, equally, it is not always easy to identify which among all the data, information, and documents are records, and therefore require special measures of control.

A high profile court case in the United States in the 1990s brought this other aspect of the problem into bold relief. *Armstrong v. Executive Office of the President,* known as the PROFS case, showed that it was difficult to distinguish records from other types of recorded information stored in electronic systems.[7] The case began in 1989 when Scott Armstrong, the executive director of a public interest organization called the National Security Archive, sought an injunction to prevent destruction of backup tapes of the electronic mail system of the Executive Office of the President (EOP) during Ronald Reagan's presidency. The lawsuit claimed that the information in the IBM Professional Office System (PROFS) qualified as records under either the Federal Records Act or the Presidential Records Act. It also claimed that the EOP failed to institute guidelines or rules in keeping with the requirements of those laws. Finally, it claimed that the Archivist of the United States failed to carry out his statutory responsibility with respect to the disposition of the electronic records in the system.

In arguments before the court, the government claimed that the PROFS was not a recordkeeping system and so did not contain records. It also argued that once electronic records were copied to paper, they no longer were records. The court rejected both claims. In effect, it said that at least some of the messages in the PROFS system were indistinguishable in purport and content from letters or memoranda, common types of records of organizations like governments. It also maintained that paper printouts are not identical copies of electronic information. Paper printouts often lack information, such as the names of all the recipients of a message, found in the electronic version. In effect, the court found these lacking elements to be vital to an understanding of the context of the record and to determination of the authenticity of the paper copies. The findings of the court raise an important question addressed by our research. What in principle are the elements essential to a record and to its proper management in the electronic environment? Knowing the answer to that question also identifies the criteria for determining what is and what is not an electronic record.

Hence, by the time our project began, it was already widely recognized in administrative, legal, and scholarly research circles that it is essential to distinguish records from other kinds of electronic documents in order to manage them in such a way as to ensure their trustworthiness. This need is especially pressing in the electronic environment because of the ease with which electronic documents can be manipulated and changed, often without leaving any adequate trace of how they have been altered and by whom. With that in mind, the project articulated the following set of objectives.

- to establish what a record is in principle and how it can be recognized in an electronic environment
- to determine what kind of electronic systems generate electronic records
- to formulate criteria that allow for the appropriate segregation of records from all other types of information in electronic systems generating and/or storing a variety of data aggregations
- to define the conceptual requirements for guaranteeing the reliability and authenticity of records in electronic systems
- to articulate the administrative, procedural and technical methods for the implementation of those requirements
- to assess those methods against different administrative, juridical, cultural, and disciplinary points of view

The first four objectives address the central theoretical underpinnings of the research. In order to distinguish a record from other sorts of documentation it is necessary to establish what a record is *in principle* and how it can be recognized in the electronic environment. The first task of the research addressed this issue. The initial results of this aspect of the work were framed in a number of templates that stated the basic concepts and hypotheses of the project. The templates were discussed and published as an appendix to the first article reporting on the project.[8] They are reproduced in Appendix A.

The first four templates define the necessary and sufficient components of

- a traditional record;
- a traditional record that is complete;
- a traditional record that is reliable; and
- a traditional record that is authentic.

The last four templates hypothesize the necessary and sufficient components of

- an electronic record;
- a complete electronic record;
- a reliable electronic record; and

- an authentic electronic record.

Over the course of the first months of the project, we tested the templates in different cultural and juridical environments. We chose to examine records keeping in Sweden and the Netherlands where there has been a strong and pervasive tradition of registration and classification. We also examined the situation in governments and private bodies in North America and in international organizations such as the World Bank and International Monetary Fund. As these investigations unfolded and as the rest of the work on the project progressed, we made refinements in our conceptualization. The final results of work pursuant to the first objective appear in Chapter 1 of this book on "The Concept of Electronic Record."

The work to establish what a record is in the electronic environment sets the project apart from other research into the policies, technical standards, and requirements for the management and preservation of electronic records in specific juridical and administrative environments. The aims of the project assume that policies, standards, and requirements for the management and preservation of trustworthy electronic records cannot be properly designed if the entities concerned are not clearly determined and recognizable. Therefore, a principal aim is to identify and define in a theoretical way both the byproducts of electronic systems and the methods for protecting the integrity of those that constitute evidence of action. While we use a deductive method to seek out all the facts common to all instances of the entities considered, most other research on electronic records uses the inductive method to gather data about reality and analyze it as a means of building generalizations.[9] We also work on the assumption that characterization of universally acceptable principles and methods of control for electronic records could only come from the application of principles and concepts already widely accepted and used to manage current records in the traditional environment.

These principles and concepts come mainly from diplomatics and archival science. While diplomatics studies records as individual, self-contained entities, archival science studies them as aggregations, analyses the functional and documentary relationships among records, and studies the ways in which records, with all their relations, can be controlled and communicated. The two perspectives are needed because electronic records can so easily be dismembered and altered; therefore, it is necessary to understand the nature and purpose of both their elemental components using the concepts of diplomatics and their aggregations in dossiers, series, and fonds using the concepts of archival science.

An important part of the initial phase of conceptualization of the project led us to refine the concept of integrity. For our purposes, we broke integrity down into two concepts, reliability and authenticity. We posited that preserving the integrity of records means ensuring that they are created reliable and maintained authentic. The meaning of reliability and authenticity was derived from diplomatic concepts. Reliability was taken to refer to the authority and trustworthiness of records as proof and memory of the activity of which they constitute the natural byproduct. A reliable record is essentially one having the capacity to stand for the facts it is about. Authenticity was taken to refer to the maintenance of a record's reliability through its transmission across time and space, its use, and its preservation over time. A record is authentic when it can be proved to be that which it is claimed to be at some point in time after its creation, whether days or centuries later. Our thinking about the concepts of reliability and authenticity of electronic records appears in Chapter 2.

By contrast, the last two objectives of the project focused on defining the conceptual requirements for guaranteeing reliability and authenticity of records actively being used in electronic systems, and articulating administrative, procedural, and technical methods for the implementation of those requirements. In pursuing these aims, we were greatly assisted by a fortuitous collaboration that, quite unexpectedly, came our way. In the summer of 1994, just as the project was getting under way, Captain Daryll Prescott, then Senior Analyst and Program Director of the Records Management Task Force of the United States Department of Defense (RMTF) approached us to express an interest in working with us. The RMTF was seeking to develop requirements for computerized support systems for the effective management of both electronic and non-electronic records. Without much difficulty, the two parties came to see a mutual interest in interpreting the theoretical concepts of our project through modeling techniques familiar to the members of the RMTF. Joining Captain Prescott on the RMTF team were Colonel Mark Kendall, who had overall responsibility for the RMTF, Mr. Edward Wyse, a consultant with expertise in modeling and business process reengineering, and Dr. William E. Underwood, an expert in artificial intelligence then on contract to the Department of Defense. Later, Dr. Kenneth Thibodeau joined the DoD team as a representative of the National Archives of the United States. Although from time to time others, who are recognized in the acknowledgements, joined in the effort briefly as opportunity permitted, it was essentially Prescott, Wyse, Underwood, Thibodeau and the authors who conducted the modeling exercise and wrote the rules governing electronic recordkeeping. For the sake of convenience, we will refer to this group as the team.

The team began work together in mid-1994 to construct models of the activities and entities involved in the management of an agency's records in an electronic system. The templates provided the starting point for the modeling exercise. The final versions of the activity models are reproduced in Appendix B and the entity model in Appendix E. A preface to the models explains how to read them. They must be read in conjunction with the Glossary, which is a necessary instrument developed during the modeling exercise. The Glossary is reproduced in Appendix C. In several cases, we decided to augment the models by designing rules to guide anyone interested in using the models to manage electronic records. These rules, as related to the models, are reproduced in Appendix D. Chapters 3 and 4 report the results of our work, as aided by the modeling exercise, to define conceptual requirements for guaranteeing reliability and authenticity and articulate administrative, procedural, and technical methods to implement them. These two chapters also explain the significance for reliability and authenticity of the rules reproduced in Appendix D.

It is particularly important to understand the perspective of our modeling work. Because we aimed to develop a conceptual model of requirements for guaranteeing the integrity of electronic records in any juridical, administrative, or organizational context, we adopted the comprehensive perspective of an entire agency, like, for example, the United States Department of Defense. It is quite possible, however, to see our work from the perspective of an entire organization, such as an industrial enterprise, an educational institution, a hospital, or a municipality. We began with the assumption that organizations and agencies would be concerned to manage all their electronic and non-electronic records in a common, coordinated fashion. We therefore adopted the perspective of such a large bureaucratic entity. We recognize, of course, that administrations or bureaucracies are more or less decentralized. The problem McDonald identified, in effect that every officer is often a solitary record-keeper, is the ultimate in decentralization. In fact, in the effort to give each officer the capacity to access and manage information using a computer, the intention was not to decentralize records to that ultimate degree, but in the worst cases of neglect of proper recordkeeping it had that very effect. In such a situation, the print-to-paper-and-file solution is little more than a desperate attempt to maintain the values of traditional recordkeeping in the computer age. It is an old story of the slow collapse of one social practice (traditional recordkeeping) and its replacement with another (electronic recordkeeping.) Nevertheless, our assumption is that traditional values, concepts, and procedures can usefully inform the new social practice of electronic recordkeeping.

Because we adopted the perspective of an agency, however, does not mean that our work cannot be applied to a smaller administrative entity, such as a branch or division of an agency or a single office. The results, if you like, are scaleable. Ultimately, any organization or agency will benefit from having consistent records practices across the whole of its branches and offices. To do this, as many archival writers have observed, is a major challenge, but it is not primarily a technical challenge. For instance, over ten years ago, based on his experience of the management of electronic records in the government of the State of New York, Alan Kowlowitz observed that "the most pressing issues ... today are not narrowly technical and methodological but broad program development and information management issues." As he put it, "policies and procedures are needed to overcome the tendency for every user to become 'an information manager,' deciding how to set up his or her electronic filing systems, what information to store there, and how long to keep it." He concluded that "an integrated system for managing electronic records was needed on an agency wide basis."[10]

When we say that the results of our work are scaleable to any administrative entity in a large bureaucracy, we do not mean that they can be lifted and placed in their totality in any particular setting. Because we take a comprehensive perspective and examine the various aspects of the problem in a conceptually coherent fashion, based on familiar principles and records-keeping practices, we feel that our recommendations can be implemented incrementally as the situation requires, to reach the goal of an organization- or agency-wide solution. It is up to the reader to see how the results of our research apply to any particular circumstance where electronic records have to be managed.

Kowlowitz also observed that "progress in addressing [electronic records] issues has been glacial." In part that has been so because organizations themselves and the information technology industry that supplies support for their business process reengineering have not had any comprehensive sense of how to solve the problem. A decade ago, this was understandable since the technology of networks, including the Internet, was in its infancy. Today, the technology exists to implement organization-wide solutions to electronic recordkeeping problems. The more important matter is to show organizations and the information technology sector what they need to do to create an environment conducive to the integrated management of both electronic and non-electronic records. To do that, comprehensive understanding of electronic records and records systems, as opposed to other material kept in other systems, needs to penetrate both the organizational and technological domains.

In summary, then, this book reports the results of basic archival research on the nature of records in electronic form and on the conceptual requirements for guaranteeing their reliability and authenticity. It is not a recipe book, but rather an investigation and presentation of a scheme of ideas to foster understanding of the nature of electronic records and the concepts and principles to be applied as the basis of their proper management.

Chapter 1
The Concept of Electronic Record
By Luciana Duranti

In coming to terms with what an electronic record is the first objective is to establish what a record is in principle and how it can be recognized in an electronic environment. The method chosen to reach this objective consists in identifying a set of general concepts on the nature of records and analyzing them in the context of the electronic environment. The general concepts are taken from diplomatics and archival science and then harmonized in a cohesive whole. The analysis of those concepts generates hypotheses that constitute the theoretical basis for establishing, among other things, whether the traditional definition of record holds true in the electronic environments.[1] It should be noted at the outset that *records* is a synonym for the term *archival documents*, which is the primary term used in diplomatics and in Latin languages for the entity in question.[2]

1.1 THE CONCEPT OF RECORD IN DIPLOMATICS

Diplomatics deals with the concept of archival document--or record--in the singular, because its analysis is carried out at the item level. This approach suits the first aim of identifying those elementary components of the individual record that an electronic system must be able to recognize. It also suits the functionality of electronic systems, which must control the entities within a system at the item level. The diplomatic definition of archival document refers to it as "the written evidence of a fact having a juridical nature, compiled in compliance with determined forms, which are meant to provide it with full faith and credit."[3] Thus, a record presents three fundamental requisites. It is written, that is, affixed to a medium in an objectified and syntactic (i.e., governed by rules of arrangement) way. It has a relationship with a fact taken into consideration by the juridical system within which it is produced.[4] It is compiled in a pre-established and controlled form aimed to ensure its trustworthiness.

As it happened, diplomatics developed in order to assess the authority and capacity of centuries-old documents to prove the existence of patrimonial rights of the church. The diplomatic wars were fought in courts, where the reliability and authenticity of old titles and privileges as proof of territorial jurisdictions was questioned. Thus, the diplomatic definition of record was directly influenced by the legal perspective, and appropriately so. In jurisprudence, and consequently in evidence laws, evidence is not an entity, but a relationship. It is the relationship shown to the trier of a fact--a judge or a jury--between the fact to be proven and the fact that proves it.[5] At the time in which the diplomatic definition of record was conceived, the facts to be proven were relatively straightforward. The records embodied the essence and substance of the facts (that is, the record itself was the fact) or constituted the required proof of the facts' existence.[6]

In the nineteenth century, diplomatics began to be considered an auxiliary science of history. When its teaching moved from the faculties of law to those of arts, the original definition of record still held true, even if there was a subtle shift from the term evidence to the term testimony or witness. The reason why historical and philological disciplines maintained the traditional diplomatic definition of record is that they regarded records primarily as sources, as the potential proof of the hypothetical fact construed by the researcher's quest to understand the past. In the mind of the scholar, in fact, there is a very specific relationship between the fact to be uncovered and the document revealing it.

However, in considering the creation of electronic records, one does not look at a record retrospectively as either proof of a given fact or a source bringing conviction of the truth of its statements. Thus, one has to consider the definition provided by archival science.

1.2 THE CONCEPT OF RECORD IN ARCHIVAL SCIENCE

Archival science shares with diplomatics very similar purposes, although it has always looked at records as aggregations, rather then as individual items. This approach also suits the aim of identifying the nature of the aggregations that an electronic system must be able to recognize. The first archival definitions of records predate the first diplomatic treatise,[7] but they clearly referred to records as sources of proof of rights, which supported arguments in disputes that otherwise would have to be solved by force.[8] Since then, archival science has consistently looked at records as sources, retrospectively, from the point of view of all subsequent users, just like diplomatics. From this perspective, to define records as evidence is accurate, because they are used as such in relation to specific research questions. However, when records are not examined in relationship to a claim or offer that is to be proven, but are considered in relation to their creator and their creation, to define them as evidence is in conflict with their purposes and undermines their potential use as evidence.[9]

Therefore, it is necessary to establish what an electronic record is in principle, independently of its possible uses, and even independently of whether it is complete or not, reliable or not, authentic or not, or destined for continuing preservation for one minute, one year, one century. The reason is that the preservation of the integrity of an entity depends on the identification, *made at the time of its creation*, of what it is that one aims to preserve, and on the analysis of how this entity changes over time in the course of being used. Rather than proceeding directly to analyze records in the electronic environment, it will be useful to determine first what a traditional record is in principle. Even though diplomatic and archival definitions adopt a different perspective from that taken in examining the integrity of electronic records, this circumstance was not regarded as implying a rejection of the diplomatic or archival theories. On the contrary, these theories are essential to understanding the nature of the entity in question.

1.3 THE ESSENTIAL ELEMENTS OF A RECORD

At the core of diplomatics lies the idea that all records can be analyzed, understood and evaluated in terms of a system of formal elements that are universal in their application and decontextualized in nature. The essential assumptions of diplomatics are that both the administrative and the documentary context of a record's creation are made manifest in its form and that this form can be separated from, and examined independently of, its content. Thus, diplomatists view records as entities embodying a system of both external and internal elements: **acts**, which are the determinant cause of record creation; **persons**, who concur in record formation; **procedures**, which are the means by which acts are carried out; and record **form**, which binds all the elements together.[10] The understanding of these elements and of their relations is necessary to recognize the entity record among all sorts of information, even when its nature and its existence are not immediately obvious. Moreover, their proper definition and translation into elements identifiable by an electronic system has the potential of facilitating their management within a recordkeeping system.

At the core of archival science is the idea that every record is linked to all the records belonging in the same aggregation by a network of relationships, which finds its expression in the *archival bond*.[11] The **archival bond** is *originary*, because it comes into existence when a record is created;[12] *necessary*, because it exists for every record (i.e., a document can be considered a record only if and when it acquires an archival bond); and *determined*, because it is qualified by the function of the record in the documentary aggregation in which it belongs. The archival bond first arises when a record is set aside and thereby connected to another in the course of action. However, it is incremental, because, as the connective tissue that joins a record to those surrounding it, it is in continuing formation and growth, until the aggregation in which the record belongs is no longer subject to expansion, that is, until the activity producing the aggregation is completed. The understanding of the archival bond and of its changes in the course of the activity in which the records participate is necessary to formulate methods of records creation, handling and preservation that protect the records' natural dynamism as well as their authenticity. With electronic records, this understanding also allows us to identify means of representing the records' relationships in a way that an electronic system will be able to recognise and maintain them intact.[13]

On the basis of the diplomatic and archival concepts discussed so far, we may define a record as any document created by a physical or juridical person in the course of practical activity as an instrument and a by-product of it. In the context of this definition, every term is provided with a very specific meaning. The term "document" refers to recorded information, where "information" is an aggregation of data[14] intended for communication to bridge space and/or time,[15] and "recorded" means affixed to a medium in a form that is objectified and governed by rules of arrangement. The verb "created" means made or received and retained[16] as the basis for further action or for reference. The term "person" refers to any entity capable of having rights or duties. A "physical person" is any human being capable of acting legally, while a "juridical person" is any collection or succession of human beings, such as an organization, a committee, or a position. A "practical activity" is a set of acts the goal of which is other than the accomplishment of the activity itself, where "acts" are manifestations of will aimed to a specific purpose.[17] Having defined what we mean by "record," we may now look at the makeup of a record.

1.4 THE COMPONENTS OF A RECORD IN THE ELECTRONIC ENVIRONMENT

The necessary and sufficient components of a record are: *medium, physical form, intellectual form, persons, action, context, archival bond, and content.* On the basis of the definition of a record in the traditional environment, we may define electronic record as any record created in a physical form that is electronic. In order to understand the analogies and differences between traditional records and electronic records, the necessary and sufficient components of the former must be compared with those of the latter.

1.4.1. Medium
The **medium** of a record is the physical carrier of the message. In traditional records, the message is inextricably affixed to the stone, clay, parchment, paper, or film supporting it, and the way it appears on the medium cannot be altered without changing the record itself. Because of this physical unbreakable link, the medium has often been imbued with meaning contributing to the message. For example, in the Papal chancery, a special kind of parchment exclusively used for writing privileges came to be identified with the privileges themselves. In scarcely literate societies, the medium of a record has been and is still used to indicate its importance (i.e., the importance of the action that it carries out), its provenance, its authority, its completion, or the type of action it participate into. Moreover, if one takes the retrospective view and looks at records as sources, one could ask several questions of a given record's medium, mostly related to date, environmental conditions, use, type of creator, kind of activity, state of perfection (for example, a draft would be on a cheaper material than an original), and so on. However, if one takes the contemporary viewpoint of a modern records creator, then one realises that the medium is not meant to convey meaning per se, but has the exclusive purpose of providing a support for the message.

With electronic records, besides being neutral as to meaning, the medium can be physically separated from the message without altering in any way the other components of the record itself. While even an electronic record cannot be said to exist if it is not affixed to a medium, the neutral character of the medium chosen to hold it, and the fact that separation does not affect any other diplomatic or archival element of the record are vital to its survival. In fact, all media that carry magnetically or optically affixed signals have very limited longevity, due partly to the deterioration of the material, but primarily to the obsolescence of the technology necessary to access and read them. The preservation of electronic records thus requires periodical reproduction for an unlimited number of times.

If the medium were meant to convey on its own meaning that contributes to the meaning of the message, each reproduction of the record would be a simple transcription of its content, with notable loss of information and authority. But if the medium is only meant to provide physical support to the record, although a necessary one, then each record reproduction in which the only component that changes is the medium can be taken to be a complete and effective record identical to the one that it reproduces.

1.4.2. Physical Form

The **form** of a record comprises the rules of representation that allow for the communication of its content. It can be distinguished into physical and intellectual form.[18] The **physical form** of a record is constituted of the formal attributes of the record that determine its external make-up. Its components are the script, type font, format, inserts, colours, language, special signs,[19] seals of any kind, etc. With electronic records, it includes the configuration and architecture of the electronic operating system, the architecture of electronic records, the software, all those parts of the technological framework that determine what the document will look like and how it will be accessed, and digital signatures and time-stamps. In electronic systems, most components of the record's physical form are invisible to the user, although several are easily identifiable. These formal elements are not item specific but category specific; that is, they are common to the same type of record. For example, within the same record making context, all confidential records will be protected by the same means, all documents linked to comments will be flagged with the same symbol, all memos will have a line separating the message from the contextual information, and all attachments will be encoded the same way.

The elements of a record's physical form are intended to convey meaning; therefore any small change would generate a new and different record. When digital technology becomes obsolescent and the records it has generated are moved to a new system to keep them accessible, several parts of their physical form are altered. This happens because the transfer of records from a technology to another presenting a different configuration is a phenomenon much more invasive than reproduction. The name itself of this operation, migration, conveys the idea that drastic change of environment largely influences the character of the migrated entity and its features, although not necessarily the apparent ones. While copying is reproduction of both the content and formal elements of the records (e.g., microfilming, photocopying, or transferring the same strings of bits from a magnetic tape to another), migration is a reproduction of the content of the record only, with both addition and loss of information. After migration, the resulting records may be made to look like the ones that have been migrated, but their physical form has substantially changed, and no trace has remained of what alteration(s) have occurred, unless the individual doing the operation has observed and taken note of them. Migration does not occur only between digital technologies: it may occur also between a digital technology and a non-digital one. The paper printout of an electronic message, for example, is a form of migration comparable to the scanning of paper documents within an electronic system.

1.4.3. Intellectual Form

The **intellectual form** of a record is the sum of its formal attributes that represent and communicate the elements of the action in which the record is involved and of its immediate context, both documentary and administrative. Intellectual form comprises three parts. **Content configuration** is the mode of expression of the message, whether text, graphic, image, sound, or a combination thereof. **Content articulation** includes the elements of the discourse (such as date, addressee, salutation) and their arrangement. **Annotations** are the additions made to a record after its compilation. Annotations can be made during the development of the procedure, to support decision making (such as mention of subsequent actions or their outcome); during the conclusive phase of a documentary action, to enable a record to carry out its purpose (such as authentication of signatures); during the course of handling the matter, to facilitate it (such as indication of "urgent" or "bring forward," date and name of action taken, or instructions for the handling office); or while managing the record, to establish and maintain intellectual and/or legal control over the record (such as classification code, registry number). Content articulation and annotations are the components of intellectual form that require the most detailed control.

Diplomatists have traditionally believed that the content articulation of a record follows a predictable pattern, which can be captured in a model, in a typical ideal document comprised of all the elements that a record at any time or place can be expected to have. Of course, this model was built on the basis of textual records, because records presenting other configurations were not very common until this century, other then perhaps graphics, which would however exist as attachments to or as inserts in textual records, thus deriving their authority, reliability and authenticity from them. The elements of such a model tended to be grouped according to a standard structure, constituted of three consecutive physical areas. The **protocol** is the top part of the document and is destined to contain its administrative context (such as date, place, persons, matter). The **text** is the central part, the body, of the document, and includes statement of the action (such as its reasons, or preamble; its background, or narration; and its content, or disposition), and related conditions and clauses. The **eschatocol** is the bottom part of the document, and is meant to contain its validation and documentary context (i.e., the mention of the means used to validate the document, or corroboration; the signature, or attestation; and the titles and responsibilities of the signing authority, or qualification of signature), together with complimentary clauses.[20]

With electronic records that are an analogue of traditional records, such as a letter or memorandum, the fundamental structure of the record remains the same. As with traditional records, in the absence of explicit contextual data in the upper portion of the document, one says that the protocol is empty. In the absence of explicit validating data in the lower portion, one says that the eschatocol is also empty. Thus, a record may have only text, and yet maintain its basic partition. Moreover, if elements that are usually contained in the eschatocol, for example, are found in the protocol, the former space does not take the name of the latter, but the anomaly is noted. Instead, when we are dealing with electronic records that do not have a paper analogue, the typical structure, although still existing, may be considerably altered or only apparently so. For example, in electronic mail messages, the header contains mention of the sender and recipient and other persons party to the message, which help set the message in its juridical administrative context and serve as means of validating it.

However, with electronic records, most elements of protocol and eschatocol exist as dictionary metadata, that is as data providing the substantial meaning of the data included in the document. In many document-making systems, metadata are usually invisible to the user, thus they can hardly be considered an intrinsic part of the record. They are more likely to be considered as a set of records themselves.[21] The situation would be quite different in recordkeeping systems, where the metadata could be inextricably linked to the record to which they refer and acquire, among others, the traditional function of protocol and eschatocol. The best way of doing so and of making the metadata accessible to users is to create a record profile for every record created in the electronic environment.

The **record profile** is an electronic form that is generated when a user tries to send or to close an electronic record. It should contain all the elements of intellectual form necessary to uniquely identify a record and place it in relation to other records belonging in the same aggregation. If so designed, it can represent the conceptual place where the administrative-documentary procedure joins with intellectual form, and where all components of intellectual form converge together. Depending on whether a record is made or received, the profile of the record could contain its date, the date and time of its receipt, the date and time of its transmission (either across space or across time, i.e., to the system itself), the archival date (i.e., the date in which the record becomes part of a dossier or series), the names and addresses of all persons participating in its creation (author, addressee, etc.), the action or matter, possible attachments, records identifier, security protection type and means, and other elements required by the specific creator or activity. If the record profile is generated for each record belonging in the same documentary aggregation, independently of medium, it could also represent the place where the components of a record (i.e. medium, physical and intellectual form, persons, act, context, content and archival bond) are explicitly described and controlled. The way in which the record profile can be implemented will be discussed in Chapter 3.

1.4.4. Persons

The most important components that need to be made evident in the records profile are the persons. Physical or juridical persons produce records.[22] **Physical persons** are human beings or natural persons, that is, persons having natural rights and duties. **Juridical persons** are collections or successions of natural persons having the capacity to act legally in the context of the enacted law or system of rules peculiar to any one people, such as an organization (collection) or a position (succession).[23]

For centuries, diplomatists have held that, while many persons may take part in the creation of a record (among them, witnesses and countersigners), only three persons are necessary to its existence. They are the *author*, the *addressee*, and the *writer*. The **author** is the person competent, that is, having the authority and capacity, for generating the record, which is issued by it, by its command, or in its name. The author of the record may coincide with the author of the action in which the record participates, or it may not. For example, a last will may be issued by the testator or by its lawyer. In the former case, the testator is the author of both the action and the record. In the latter, the testator is the author of the action, while the author of the record is the lawyer. The **addressee** is the person for whom the record is intended. It may or may not coincide with the person to whom the action is directed or the record is delivered. For example, with a patent for an invention, the addressee of the record is "all those who are concerned," while the addressee of the action is the inventor, to whom the record is also delivered. The same person may be author and addressee of the same record, as in a contract and in every other record resulting from an act of reciprocal obligation. This also happens when a person directs a record to himself. The **writer** is the person responsible for the intellectual form of the record. Every time a record is authored by an abstract entity such as a corporation, organization or state, the writer is the juridical person who takes the initiative and responsibility for compiling the record.[24]

Although a record taken individually presents only three necessary persons, archival scholars believe that each record must also be seen in the context of its network of relationships, the most important of which is the one it has with its creator. The **creator** of a record is the person that generates the highest-level aggregation in which the record belongs, that is, the fonds. A **fonds** is the whole of the records that a physical or juridical person naturally accumulates by reason of its activities and as byproducts of them.[25] With administrative change today as with territorial change in the past, the creator is not always easily identified with the person to whom the series and file belonged when a given record was made or received and included in them. However, when one is confronted with a traditional record, the physical presence of a record in a given aggregation of records leads to the reasonable assumption that the creator of the record is the same as the creator of the whole aggregation. It is not always so with electronic records. If a given record exists in a live system, where it is associated with a specific group of records, one can safely make a similar assumption. The creator would be the person using the system for making, receiving and accumulating records in the conduct of business. But, once the record is taken out of the system, and preserved on some magnetic or optical support, its location on a storage medium and in a given storage facility is no longer meaningful for the purpose of identifying its creator. Thus, it is necessary to find means of permanently associating the identity of a record creator with all the records that it creates. The most likely means of doing so seems to be the record profile. In an ideal system, the identity of the creator of an electronic record would be revealed by a visual or presentation component of the record profile attached as an annotation to each record item, such as a logo or a crest.

This is not only true for the creator, though. The need to control each and every electronic record makes it necessary to keep track of a multiplicity of persons involved in their creation and maintenance. Besides the creator, the **originator** also needs to be identified for each electronic record made or received and set aside for action or reference. The originator is the person owning the address where the record has been generated (i.e., from which the record is sent or in where the record is compiled and kept). The primary reason for this identification is that the originator may be different from the author or writer of the record, especially when a record has multiple authors but only one of them is responsible for its transmission: the issue relates primarily to responsibility and accountability. The identity of the originator of an electronic mail message is in its header, while that of the originator of the other types of records is in the metadata, but its most appropriate place is again the record profile.

1.4.5. Action
The core component of every record, regardless of its medium and form, is the **action**. An action is any exercise of will that aims to create, change, maintain or extinguish situations.[26] Any record owes its existence to the fact that it participates in some action. All actions fall into one of two categories: those for which the initiative belongs to the person or persons who carry them out and those for which the initiative belongs to another person. Actions can be further classified according to the will carrying them out, the persons to whom they are addressed, the way in which they develop, or the function they are meant to accomplish. These types of classifications will be discussed in the context of the design of business procedures. What is relevant to the understanding of the nature of records in general, and electronic records in particular, and thus important to examine in the context of the components of a record, is the relationship that a record has with the action in which it participates.

This relationship is usually revealed by the conceptual position that the record occupies in the aggregation of records to which it is connected by a classification code or any other means. A record may be the essence of the action carried out by the creator, which comes into existence with the creation of the record. In such a case, the record is said to be generated *ad substantiam* because, being the substance of the act, it coincides with it. For example, the drawing up of a contract substantiates an action of sale; or the entering of the relevant data in the patients' database substantiates the action of admitting a patient in a hospital. This type of record is called *dispositive*. Alternatively, a record may not be necessary for carrying out the action, but may be generated *ad probationem*, that is, in order to provide proof that the action took place. This existence of written proof must be a legal requirement, not a choice of the creator. For example, marriage, being an oral act, does not need a record for it to take place, but does require a record, the registration, as proof that it took place. This type of record is termed *probative*. Other examples of probative records are the accident reports entered by an insurance officer in the organization's database, and an electronic list of registered voters. In the cases of both dispositive and probative records, the written form of the action is required by the juridical system.[27]

The records whose written form is not required may be generated as a means for acting or as a support for action. In the former case, they are called *narrative* records, and in the latter *supporting* records. Narrative records are those that carry out and therefore are the substance of actions of non-legal consequences. They do not relate to business activity other than by being expression of the way in which individuals set themselves to work and go through the informal motions of carrying out activities and decision-making. While they are records themselves, they are not procedurally bound to action in the way in which the other types of records are, but relate to it in a very indirect way. Much electronic mail fits the category of narrative records very clearly.

Supporting records are those that help to carry out an oral action. Examples are teaching notes and informal meeting agenda (i.e., those the written form of which is not required by the juridical system). The major part of electronic records has a supporting function with respect to the action in which they take part. For example, a geographical informational system (i.e., a relational database which presents data in a geographic arrangement, contains only documents,[28] information,[29] or individual data[30]. However, the geographical information system itself can be considered a record, if its function as a database is to support a specific business activity, because it does have all the necessary components of a record when it is regarded as a unit. Moreover, it can produce documents that, once extracted from it and linked to other records of action, become records, for example, a representation of the intensity of traffic in a given place that is attached to a report containing recommendations for the regulation of city traffic.

1.4.6. Context

Context is the necessary component of the record whose meaning is the most difficult to define, because, if not qualified by an attribute, the term refers to anything outside the record that has significance for its meaning. It is essential to specify at each given time what context one is referring to, if one wishes to use the concept in a meaningful way. Every record has four relevant contexts. The *juridical-administrative context* is the legal and organizational system in which the records creating body belongs, which establishes the parameters within which the capacity and authority to act of the creator occur. The *provenancial context* is the records creating body, its mandate, structure and functions. The *procedural context* is the procedure[31] in the course of which a record is generated. The *documentary context* is constituted by the fonds in which the record belongs and its internal structure.[32] If one proceeds from the first to the last context, one may note a progression from the general to the specific. The closer a context gets to the record, the more important it is to its meaning. Thus, documentary context is vital to the understanding of every record.

Some consider "technological context" as one of increasing relevance. If, by technological context, one refers to the technology generating determined groups of records, it is quite clear that such technology conditions and penetrates their form and is therefore a component of the records rather than of their context. If instead one refers to the technological characteristics of the recordkeeping system containing the records, it is difficult to see how it could be looked at separately from the records documentary context. For example, a concern of those who speak of technological context is represented by "shared databases," which contain documents, information, or data accessible to many persons. The fact is, however, that these databases do not contain "shared electronic records," because each database can only be the responsibility of one juridical person (and this can be a consortium of persons). Each juridical person who uses material contained in a shared database in the course of its own activity generates with it in its own electronic system its own electronic records.[33]

1.4.7. Archival Bond

Ultimately, the key to the existence of an electronic record is the **archival bond**, without which a record would not exist. Differently from the context, the archival bond is not external to the record, but an integral part of it. It contains within itself the direction of the cause-effect relationship, and it is therefore the primary expression of the development of the activity in which the document participates, rather than of the act that the document embodies (e.g., appointment, grant, or application). Therefore, it is a principal determinant of the meaning of the record. [34] The archival bond, which is the intellectual link between a record and the record that immediately precedes and/or follows it, conceptually arises at the moment in which a document that has been made or received is set aside for action or reference, rather than being discarded. The arising of the bond determines the moment of the creation of the record.[35] Because the bond between two records comes into existence when the connection between them is established, with traditional records, this bond is implicit in the physical arrangement of the records. With electronic records, it can only be manifested in the specific classification code assigned to the record, which connects it to other records belonging to the same class. In a proper electronic recordkeeping system, the classification code would be included as an annotation in the record profile, thereby fixing the record's relations and stabilizing them at the point of its incorporation into the central record system. In systems that are not designed specifically for keeping records, the filing identifier would be part of the metadata that constitute the data dictionary.

1.4.8. Content

The final component of a record is its **content**, that is the textual, symbolic, and/or or visual message that is meant to be conveyed. For a record to exist at all as a definite, distinct, and identifiable entity, its content must be fixed and stable. This is the norm with traditional records, where the content cannot be separated either from its form or from the medium to which it is affixed. With electronic records, content, form and medium can exist separately. Parts of the content can also be scattered in various areas of the digital memory and even in different applications, databases, and so on. Moreover, those scattered parts can be changed quite independently the one from the other, and even without human intervention, if one or more of them happen to belong in a fluid, constantly up-to-date database, for example. Documents consisting of pointers to data residing in different locations within a database, or in multiple databases are called "virtual documents" and cannot be considered records, in the electronic environment. It is quite possible and normal to see them on a computer screen as entire unified documents. However, they do not exist as such until their components are actually joined together in an inextricable way, that is, until the content of the document is explicitly articulated in a fixed form. This is different from what happens with traditional records, where a document constituted of pointers to information contained in other documentary sources is a record of the sources to be used to make another record.[36] With electronic documents, the pointers lead to data that, being contained in databases susceptible to changes, may vary overtime. Thus, a virtual document lacks stability and may be ten different documents in a short time span.

The fact that all the components identified and illustrated above are necessary (i.e., must all be present) and sufficient (i.e., beyond them, no other component needs to be present) for the existence of any record implies a few other requisites. These requisites are primarily related to transmission and communication. The necessary presence of an addressee in every record implies the intent of transmission. A record created with the intent of being transmitted must actually be capable of being transmitted and, at the moment of creation, must be readable and intelligible by its intended addressee.[37] Successful transmission is not necessary for a record to be made, but certainly it is for a record to be received, and the received record must be readable and intelligible at the moment of receipt. The fact that successful transmission is not necessary for a record to be made means that a record which is unable to reach the addressee is still a record in the system of the creator if it is set aside by the sender. Moreover, the notification that the record did not reach its destination is a received record in the system of the sender if it joins the sent message in the aggregation in which it belongs. Together, they constitute evidence that an action took place but could not be completed and reach its effects.

The intended transmission does not need to be over space, as it can be over time. Take, for example, ledgers or registers, which are created to bridge time. Or take, as a different example, memoranda written to oneself and filed to aid memory. In both cases, the addressee is not expressed but implied, even if in the case of ledgers and registers the addressee is intended to be whomever is concerned, while in the case of a memo to oneself the addressee is identical with the author.

1.5 CONCLUSION

All the components that have been discussed need to be present *at the same time* in a document for it to be a record. If one of them is missing, a record does not exist. The consequences of this fact for electronic records can be considered in relation to specific components. In an electronic environment, a document must be saved on a medium (e.g., hard drive, disk) at least once when compiled or received in order to be able to be considered a record. If the medium alone is then changed (e.g., the document is moved from a disk to a tape), the record does not change, because the medium only carries meaning rather than conveying it, although its status of transmission[38] varies, as any record transported from a medium to another becomes a copy of the previous record. However, a document appearing on a computer screen, but not saved in the environment of the person viewing it, is not a record in such environment (e.g., any document accessed on but not downloaded from the Internet).

It is often stated that actions and transactions may take place between electronic systems. With the advent of artificial intelligence and expert systems, it has even been suggested that their decision making power warrants considering them as persons. However, person is a legal concept, and unless the law recognizes that such systems are capable of acting legally, the quality of person can only be attributed to human beings or to entities made up of human beings, such as organizations. This implies that, when an electronic system is used, the creator, author, originator, writer and addressee, as well as all the other possible persons intervening in the production of the record (e.g., witnesses, countersigners) must be identifiable from among those individuals or bodies who use such a system. The process of identifying persons retrospectively (i.e., after the records have been generated) may be very complex when dealing with shared systems both within and across organizations. In such cases, it is necessary to analyse the competences of the various users of the system at any given time. This is one of the reasons why it is so important that access privileges be linked to competences at the moment of the design of the architecture of the electronic system, as it will be seen later on in this volume. At this time, the point to be made is that no record can exist for which the five required persons are not uniquely identifiable.

The relationship between an electronic entity (i.e., any aggregation of data) and an action is key to the determination of its record nature, because, in the absence of such relationship, there cannot be a record. For example, a student's registration for university courses carries out the action in question, a grant ledger provides evidence of actions already completed, informal messages informing of the circumstances of a given action narrate its context, and the layer of a geographic information system (GIS) attached to a memo gives support to the decision based on such view. However, a GIS layer that is not explicitly (either physically or intellectually) connected to an action is not a record, but a simple aggregate of data, although a GIS as a whole, if clearly connected to a given activity of a creator who uses it routinely as part of its business procedures, can be regarded as a supporting record.[39]

The archival bond expresses the connection of the electronic entity with a record strictly related to it via the action in which they both participate. As already mentioned, the archival bond comes into being when a documentary entity is filed (set aside in a recordkeeping system) or assigned a classificatory code that shows the intellectual connection between such entity and a record. Thus, if a document is first compiled in an electronic record-making system, and then filed, either by assigning it to a dossier or by giving to it a classificatory code, in a separate electronic recordkeeping system,[40] the document that remains in the former system is not a record, for it lacks the documentary context to give it meaning, while that in the latter is a record.

The components of records in general and of electronic records in particular as examined in this chapter constitute the conceptual basis for establishing how electronic records can be created reliable and maintained authentic. However, in order to develop the methods and procedures necessary to achieve such goal, we need to analyze the concepts of reliability and authenticity as they apply to traditional records first and as they can be extended to electronic records afterward.

Chapter 2
The Reliability and Authenticity of Electronic Records
By Luciana Duranti

The noun authenticity and the related adjective authentic have been and are still used by a variety of disciplines as all encompassing terms for several different concepts. An authentic object may be one reflecting the intentions of its maker, conforming to the practice of its maker's historical period, or having content and articulation similar or identical to those used during its maker's lifetime. Alternatively, an authentic object may be the first generated, the only one proceeding directly from the author, the original one, the prototype, as opposed to a copy, which would be inauthentic by definition. In another meaning, an authentic object is one that is fully identifiable on its face, as opposed to its context, and that somebody different from the author has the authority to declare authentic, by virtue of being either the original or a copy conforming to the original. In archival science, authenticity is a characteristic of all archival documents, which are expression of the entity producing them in the usual and ordinary course of its affairs.

> It is contingent to the facts of creation, maintenance and custody. Records are authentic only when they are created with the need to act through them in mind, and when they are preserved and maintained as faithful witnesses of facts and acts by their creator or legitimate successors. To hold authentic memorials of past activity means creating, maintaining, and keeping custody of documents according to regular procedures which can be attested.[1]

The concept of authenticity is at the heart of the diplomatic science and discipline.[2] This concept was formulated and used in the seventeenth century in direct relation to form. A document came to be considered authentic if the characteristics of its physical and intellectual form are typical of the juridical system, the time and the place (including the specific chancery, record office, or notary office) in which the document purports to have been produced. The concept of authenticity so defined included two other concepts, those of genuineness and reliability. According to diplomatic theory, if one could prove that a document is authentic, one can infer that the same document is also genuine and reliable.[3] In other words, if a document has all the formal elements that it was supposed to present when first made or received and set aside (i.e., if it is authentic), that document is what it purports to be (i.e., it is genuine), and its content can be trusted (i.e., it is reliable).

This diplomatic assumption held true at a time when the procedures, rules and routines for records creation were so rigorous, and the means of authentication so inaccessible to anyone other than the persons entitled to use them that it was practically impossible to generate documents formally correct other than in the competent chancery, records office, or notary office. This assumption cannot be considered valid anymore, particularly when electronic systems participate in record-making and recordkeeping procedures. In the introduction to a volume of writings about authenticity of electronic records, Abby Smith writes: " 'Authenticity' in recorded information connotes precise, yet disparate, things in different contexts and communities. It can mean being original, but also being faithful to an original; it can mean uncorrupted but also of clear and known provenance, 'corrupt' or not."[4]

However, the need for a clear understanding of the concept of authenticity in the digital environment is stronger than ever, because methods for preserving and testing the authenticity of electronic records must be based on such unequivocal definition. Historian Charles Cullen writes: "...scholars need to question what it is they are using ...they need to authenticate all documentation they use in the process of learning and of creating new scholarship. An authentic object is one whose integrity is intact—one that is and can be proven or accepted to be what its owners say it is."[5] And he continues, "A digital object must be authenticated at the time of its creation by a means that will convey a high degree of confidence to all users, including subsequent use by the originator."[6] He concludes: "Without a deliberate and distinctive marking caused by the author that could not be guessed by another or altered by anyone, it seems impossible to authenticate an electronic document without doubt. Authors of files or images must take steps to establish authorship of their work; if not our only option is to accept the assertions of others."[7] Obviously, Cullen makes the concept of authenticity coincide with the concept of authentication, on the assumption that the latter implies the former. In archival science and diplomatics, however, authenticity is regarded as a quality of the record, while authentication is only a means of proving that a record is what it purports to be at a given moment in time. In other words, authentication is a declaration of authenticity at a particular point in time resulting either from the insertion or the addition of an element or a statement to a record, and the rules governing it are established in law. It might enable the verification of authenticity after transmission of the record across space (either physical or virtual), but cannot allow for such verification when records are transmitted through time. The requirements for the continuing verifiable authenticity of records go much beyond legal means of authentication and even juridical principles and structures, deriving from the historical stratification of traditions, uses, attitudes, and perceptions that each culture brings to bear on what it treats as an authentic record.

Asserting the traditional archival point of view, Peter Hirtle states: "Archivists need to be able to assert, often in court, that the records in their custody were actually created by the agency specified. Furthermore, the archivist must be able to assert that the records have been in the custody only of the agency or the archives. In an analogue environment, the legal and physical transfer of the documents from the agency to the archives ensures an unbroken chain of custody.

...The archivist would not be expected to testify as to the accuracy of the contents of the records. However, he or she should be able to assert that on the day when the records left the custody of the originating agency or organization, a particular document was included as part of the records."[8] Here the meaning of authenticity is strictly limited to being what an entity purports to be on the basis of circumstantial evidence. This might create several problems with electronic records, especially considering the fact that, after being saved to a file for the first time, they are kept and used as copies. David Levy is very much concerned with this issue when he states that, if being authentic means being who or what you seem or claim to be, in some cases there might only be one right answer, but in other cases there may be more than one right answer. "Judgements of authenticity, as I understand it," he writes, "allow us to navigate through a world by distinguishing genuine multiplicity from duplicity."[9] To complicate the issue, he adds: "The definition of 'faithful'...depends on the circumstances in which the copy is being made and on the uses to which it will be put. The context of use, in other words, determines which properties of the original must be preserved in the copy."[10]

It is quite clear, from the discussion going on in the scholarly and professional communities, that, in order to ensure that contemporary records can be trusted throughout their existence, it is essential to examine the meaning of the three separate concepts of genuineness, reliability and authenticity and to identify the means necessary to guarantee that every document generated and preserved has those qualities.[11]

The concept of genuineness refers to the legitimacy of the record in its context. A genuine document is the actual intact by-product of the activity of its purported author. It can be trusted to have been produced by the competent body as an instrument of action and to have remained immune from tampering since its genesis. Genuineness cannot be directly ascertained other than by never losing sight of a given document since its compilation, but it can be indirectly ensured and tested. The two concepts that allow for the indirect assessment and verification of the genuineness of a record are those of reliability and authenticity.

2.1 RELIABILITY

Reliability refers to the authority and trustworthiness of a record as evidence of what it is about, that is, to its ability to stand for the fact it speaks of. It depends upon two things: the degree of completeness of a record's form and the degree of control exercised over the documentary procedure in the course of which the record is generated.

Records can be assessed in terms of standards other than their effectiveness in mirroring facts, that is, they can be assessed in terms of form. This evaluation amounts to redefining the *record as a visible fact at which the user is present*. If a record possesses all the various bureaucratically necessary forms and those forms are complete, the user can achieve complete passivity and treat the record as a thing which is showing him/her what it is.

> Completeness is the major standard in terms of which records are actually assessed...Completeness is the bureaucrat's way to the real.[12]

Thus, completeness refers to the fact that the record possesses all the elements of intellectual form necessary for it to be capable of generating consequences, of reaching the purpose for which it is issued. These elements include the date, the mention of the necessary persons involved in the creation of the record and of the action or matter to which the record relates, and some manifestation of its archival bond, whether a classification code or any other identifier capable of placing the record within its documentary context. The date is essential because it captures the relation between the person(s) authoring and writing the record and the fact or event to which the record relates, and makes the record speak about this relation, thereby objectifying and communicating it.[13] The persons whose mention in the intellectual form is necessary to the completeness of the record are the author and/or the writer,[14] and the addressee. The name(s) of the author and writer give(s) responsibility for the issuing of the record, its content, and its articulation and need(s) to be expressed in some sort of attestation; for example, signatures, signets, names, e-mail addresses (if appearing in an e-mail header.) This attestation functions as a declaration that the record mirrors the fact(s) it is about, and it legally establishes who is accountable for what the record says and for the record as a fact itself. The name of the addressee establishes for whom the record is intended, provides the direction of the action and of the communication, and contributes to the formation of the administrative context of the record. The mention of the action in the record manifests the reason why the record comes into existence, and the manifestation of the archival bond establishes and later reveals the network of documentary relationships of the record.

Depending on the jurisdiction within which a record is issued, and on the type of record, other elements of intellectual form may be required for the record to be able to reach its effects, such as conditional clauses or the signature of a witness. However, the elements mentioned above are necessary for any record to be considered complete. An incomplete record, if presenting all the essential components of a record,[15] is to be considered a record nevertheless. It might also be considered reliable, if it has been generated according to a controlled documentary procedure, because reliability is a question of degree: a record may be more or less reliable, rather then either reliable or unreliable.

A documentary procedure is the body of rules governing the making of an archival document. Some of these rules refer to the persons who make records. They establish who has the authority and the capacity to make (i.e., issue and/or write) and/or sign which records; who is accountable through the record for the action the record is about; and who is responsible for the existence of the record. Among them, there are rules that give responsibility to different persons for recording the same facts, so that what the resulting records have in common can be trusted to be true. There are also rules requiring that the same fact or part of it be reported at the same time to different addressees, so that the message cannot be tailored to the reader. Other rules refer to the routing of the records, specifying the workflow for the accomplishment of each action; and still others prescribe the handling of the records in the course of their compilation, completion, and filing, as this latter operation determines the record's documentary context. The more rigorous and detailed the rules, the more established the routine, the more reliable the records resulting from their application will be.

Reliability, then, is linked exclusively to record making, although one could infer the reliability of received records on the basis of their participation in the relevant business procedure. If an organization receives a record in the regular course of one of its activities, files it, acts upon it according to established routine procedures, and makes reference to it over time, it might be safely assumed that the document is reliable. However, reliability is the sole responsibility of the physical or juridical person making the record, and the lack of it cannot be blamed on the recipient of the record, notwithstanding the fact that the latter is the record creator.[16]

Reliable records result from the integration of business and documentary procedures, and from the establishment of a reliable and secure electronic system that is itself integrated within the creator's overall recordkeeping system, where a recordkeeping system is defined as

> a set of internally consistent rules that govern the making, receiving, setting aside, and handling of active and semi-active records in the usual and ordinary course of the creator's affairs, and the tools and mechanisms used to implement them. Recordkeeping is keeping records of action.

The rules governing such systems must ensure, among other things, that each record be profiled, classified, registered, and accessible only for reading purposes (as opposed to writing, editing, deleting, adding or other purposes.) The procedures and rules ensuring and supporting the maintenance of the reliability of electronic records will be presented and discussed in detail in the following chapters.

2.2 AUTHENTICITY

Authenticity is linked to the record's state, mode and form of transmission, and to the manner of its preservation and custody. A document is authentic if it can be demonstrated that it is precisely as it was when first transmitted or set aside for preservation, and if its reliability, i.e., the trustworthiness it had at that moment, has been maintained intact. Thus, authenticity is a responsibility of both the record creator (i.e., the person who sets aside the records it makes or receives), and its legitimate successor (i.e., either the body acquiring the function(s) from which those records result—and the records themselves—or the archival body competent for the preservation of its records).

Authenticity is protected and guaranteed through the adoption of methods that ensure that the record is not manipulated, altered, or otherwise falsified after its creation, either during its transmission or in the course of its handling and preservation, within both the recordkeeping system and the record-preservation system, the latter being

> a set of internally consistent rules that govern the intellectual and physical maintenance by the creator of semi-active and inactive records overtime, and the tools and mechanisms necessary to implement them.

Thus, the units within the record creator and its legitimate successor, which are competent for handling, maintaining, and preserving its records (both those made *and* received records), are accountable for the records' authenticity. Such responsibility affects the authors of the records, both those within the creator and those outside (the makers of the received records), only as their transmission is concerned.

Transmission, which diplomatics terms *traditio*, can be over space or over time. Transmission over space happens when a records crosses communication boundaries between persons, while transmission over time occurs when a record is preserved by its author for future reference by itself or another person. Typically, correspondence is meant for transmission over space, while journals, registers, and data banks are meant for transmission over time. Records can be transmitted at different stages in their formation. The *status of transmission* of a record is its degree of perfection at any given time it is taken into consideration. A record may have the status of *draft*, *original*, or *copy*. A draft is a sketch of the record made for purpose of correction. It can exist itself in various stages of completeness, so that one can have a first draft, a final draft and an undetermined number of drafts in between the two. Drafts are incapable of reaching legal consequences, and, if preserved, are usually intended for transmission only over time.[17] While drafts often constitute the most informative state of transmission retrospectively, they are the least reliable. Besides being incomplete, they are not subject to controlled documentary procedures, and are not authentic, as they do not present any of the formal elements that allow for the verification of authenticity and the consequent inference of genuiness.[18]

As it regards transmission, the methods for ensuring the authenticity of records in general, and electronic records in particular, relate to the assessment of the status of transmission of each record on the basis of the way in which transmission affects the physical and intellectual form of the record. As it regards handling and preservation, the methods for ensuring records authenticity relate to the documentation of unbroken custody, and to the existence of controlled procedures for physical preservation and of self-authenticating procedures for reproduction and migration. These methods as they concern active and semi-active records maintained by their creating agency will be discussed later. However, a few more general reflections are in order. As Clifford Lynch notes,

> There seems to be a sense that digital information needs to be held to a higher standard for authenticity and integrity than has printed information. In other words, many people feel that in an

environment characterized by pervasive deceit, it will be necessary to provide verifiable proof for claims related to authorship and integrity that would usually be taken at face value in the physical world...authenticity and integrity, when held to this standard, are elusive properties. It is much easier to devise abstract definitions than testable ones. When we try to define integrity and authenticity with precision and rigor, the definition recurses into a wilderness of mirrors, of questions about trust and identity in the networked information world.[19]

Thus, in order to distinguish the two concepts, Lynch points to the questions that need to be asked. The questions about the integrity of the object concern whether the object has been changed since its creation, and, if so, whether this has altered its fundamental essence. The questions about the authenticity of the object presuppose its integrity. If its integrity is intact, are the assertions made about the object, be they embedded within it (e.g., a formula of corroboration, or of authentication) or external to it (e.g., the related registry entry, or the metadata in a record profile), true or false? In a traditional environment, the answers to these questions can be based either on the documentation of the provenance of the object and its reliability, on the characteristics and content of the object and their consistency with the claims made about it, on signatures and seals and the claims made about them, or on the analysis of other versions of the same object.[20] In the digital environment, Lynch concludes, answers will come from the analysis of the content of the object, from formal and computational ways of evaluating signatures and seals and documentation of provenance, and from proving a chain of custody by a trusted party. In fact, the trust requirement is to him the most important:

> There are two basic strategies for testing a claim. The first is to believe the claim because we can verify its integrity and authenticate its source, and because we choose to trust the source....The second strategy is what we might call "independent verification" of the claim. For example, if there is a national author registry that we trust, we might verify that the data in the author registry are consistent with the claims of authorship. In both cases, however, validating a claim that is associated with an object ultimately means nothing more or less than making the decision to trust some entity that makes or warrants the claim.

And he adds:

> It is an interesting and possibly surprising conclusion that in the digital environment, tests of integrity can be viewed as just special cases and byproducts of evaluation of authenticity...when we are dealing with dynamic objects such as databases...there is no question of authenticity through comparison with other copies; there is only trust or lack of trust in the location and delivery processes and, perhaps, in the archival custody chain.[21]

Lynch's position is a very important one as it points us towards the very large question of devising methods of preserving and verifying the authenticity of inactive electronic records across time. Even though in this project we were not concerned with inactive records, we were always aware as we worked that good electronic recordkeeping is the necessary precondition for effective preservation of inactive electronic records. If records in the electronic environment are created and managed properly, there is good reason to suppose that we will be able to devise principles, criteria and standards for the long-term preservation of the authenticity of inactive electronic records.

Chapter 3
Methods for Creating and Maintaining Electronic Records *as* Records
By Heather MacNeil

The goal of our project was to identify and define the nature of an electronic record and the conditions necessary to ensure its reliability and authenticity during its active and semi-active life. Thus, the project's orientation was both conceptual and methodological. The conceptual work consisted of the identification of the components of a *record*, and the conditions necessary to create a *reliable and authentic record* in both paper and electronic recordkeeping environments, as detailed in the previous two chapters. The methodological work consisted of the elaboration of methods for creating and maintaining reliable and authentic electronic records based on that conceptual foundation, as detailed in this chapter and the next. This chapter examines specifically the principal methods we have identified for creating, maintaining, and retrieving electronic records *as* records (rather than as data or information), while the next one examines the principal methods for ensuring their reliability and protecting their authenticity.

The main methods for creating and retrieving electronic records as records include:

3.1   profiling records; and
3.2   retrieving records in context.

3.1 PROFILING RECORDS

3.1.1.   *Creating a record profile for every record in the records system*
The profiling of records is a key method for creating and maintaining electronic records as records, and for integrating the management of the electronic and non-electronic components of the records system. A record profile is an electronic form that is generated when an electronic record is either made or received (see Appendix D, rules A21 and A22), or in the case of non-electronic records, when the record is forwarded to the central records system. The fields included within the record profile correspond to the components and elements of a record identified in Chapter 1. The act of filling in the fields of the record profile makes explicit and formalizes the act of setting aside a record either for action or reference and establishes the record's archival bond with other records of the creator.

The purpose of a record profile is to identify a record in a unique manner and to place it in relation to other records belonging in the same aggregation.[1] It is a repository of the core elements of a record's intellectual form and context that establish the documentary, procedural and provenancial context in which the record was created and used and that attest to the fact that the record was made or received in the usual and ordinary course of business.

The profile is not only a repository of annotations; it is an annotation in itself and, as such, it is inextricably linked to the record for as long as the record exists. When a record is removed from the central records system for transfer either to semi-active storage or to a competent archival body, its profile must be removed and transferred with it. When a record is destroyed, its profile must also be destroyed with it.

Profiling records is associated not only with the creation of a record as a record; it is also contributes to a record's reliability because it contains elements that contribute to a record's completeness and constitutes part of the control exercised over records creation. It also supports an attestation of the records' authenticity because some of the specific annotations included in the profile provide information about the transmission and use of active and semi-active records. Such information is necessary to verify whether and to what extent the record has been altered since its creation.

A comprehensive list of the fields included in the record profile form follows.

Protocol number, i.e., the consecutive number assigned to each incoming or outgoing record in the protocol register. With non-electronic records, the protocol number must be copied as a management annotation onto the record.

Date of receipt, i.e., the date the record is received by the agency to which it was sent. For both electronic and non-electronic records, it corresponds to the date on which the record is assigned a protocol number.

Time of receipt, i.e., the time the record is received by the agency to which it was sent. This element is not relevant to non-electronic records, except in very specific circumstances regulated by legal requirements.

Date of transmission, i.e., the date the record leaves the space in which it was generated, either to go from one space to another or from the general space to outside the agency or from the records office to outside the agency.

Time of transmission, i.e., the time the record leaves the space in which it generated. This element is not relevant to non-electronic records, except in very specific circumstances regulated by legal requirements.

Date of record, i.e., the date assigned to it by the author. It appears in the intellectual form of the record, specifically in the content articulation.

Archival date, i.e., the date assigned to a record by the records office. For electronic records, the archival date is the date a record is received into the general space of the electronic system. For non-electronic records, the archival date is the date that appears on the date stamp affixed to the record by the records office.

Protocol number of sending office, i.e., the protocol number assigned to the record by the agency sending it. This element is only relevant in cases where the sending agency uses a protocol register to control its incoming and outgoing records.

Originator's name, i.e., the name of the person from whose electronic address the record has been sent.

Originator's address, i.e., the electronic address from which the record has been sent.

Author's name, i.e., the name of the person competent to issue the record or in whose name or by whose command the record has been issued.

Author's address, i.e., the address of the person competent to issue the record or in whose name or by whose command the record has been issued.

Writer's name, i.e., the name of the person competent for the articulation of the content of the record.

Writer's address, i.e., the address of the person competent for the articulation of the content of the record.

Action or matter, i.e., the fact that triggers the issuing of the record.

Number of attachments, i.e., the number of previously autonomous items that have been linked inextricably to the record before transmission in order for it to accomplish its purpose.

Medium, i.e., the physical carrier of the record.

Handling office, i.e., the office competent for treating a matter.

Action taken, i.e., in the case of received records, the act taken in response to the receipt of the record.

Addressee's name, i.e., the name of the person to whom the record is directed or for whom the record is intended.

Addressee's address, i.e., the address of the person to whom the record is directed or for whom the record is intended.

Receiver's name, i.e., the name of each person to whom the record is copied for information purposes.

Receiver's address, i.e., the address of each person to whom the record is copied for information purposes.

Class code of the record, i.e., that component of the classification code which corresponds to the code of the class in which the record belongs, as it appears in the classification scheme.

Dossier Identifier of the record, i.e., that component of the classification code which corresponds to the identifier for the dossier in which the record belongs. It may be constituted by the name of a person or organization, a symbol, a progressive number, a date, or a specific topic within the class's general subject.

Record Item Identifier, i.e., that component of the classification code which corresponds to the progressive number of the record within the dossier (or, in the absence of dossiers, within the specific class). This identifier is assigned to the record when it is consigned to the central records system. The record item identifier is the final component of the classification code.

Mode of transmission, i.e., the method by which a record is communicated over space or time.

Draft number, i.e., the consecutive number assigned to sequential drafts of the same record.

Depending on the type of application used, some of these fields would be filled in by the electronic system, others by the author or writer, and still others by the record office. The fact that all the fields are included on the form does not mean that every field must be filled in for every record made or received. The decision to include all or only some of the fields will be based on the creator's needs and may vary from one record type to another. It is expected that only the profiles of the records for which maximum reliability and authenticity are required would have all the fields filled in.

The procedural rules governing the record profile, however, do identify a number of fields that should be filled in to identify a record properly and place it in relation to other records. For electronic records, the fields are filled in according to the requirements established for the space (i.e., individual, group, general) in which the record is being saved or sent (see Appendix D, rule A131(j)). For example, to save a record in the individual space, the officer must record the **date of record**, the **author's name**, the **addressee's name**, and identify the **action or matter** to which the record relates in the appropriate fields of the profile. If a record made in the individual space is transmitted to another individual space, or to the group space, the officer must record, in addition, the **date and time of transmission, receiver(s) name(s), number of attachments, class code** and **dossier identifier** as applicable.

For non-electronic records, the elements of the profile are filled in according to records office procedures (see Appendix D, rule A131(e) and (k)). The procedural rules include a list of fields recommended for inclusion. Exclusive competence for profiling non-electronic records is given to the records office.

3.1.2. Creating an electronic repository of record profiles

The repository of record profiles is a tool for integrating control over all active records belonging in the same aggregation by providing a central storage location in the electronic system for the record profiles that are created for every electronic and non-electronic record. Such integrated control is necessary because a significant proportion of organizational records continue to be created and maintained in non-electronic form as textual, graphic, cartographic, and architectural records. To maintain the archival bond between records created to carry out the same activity but generated and/or stored on different media in different physical locations, those records must be connected intellectually through their profiles.

As articulated in the procedural rules governing its design, the repository is intended to serve access needs by allowing for the creation of various views of the profiles in relation to the specific dossier and class to which the record belongs. It is also intended to serve authenticity needs by allowing for the creation of a final view of the record profiles of all the records in each dossier or class before it is removed from the central records system. The creation of a final view is a way of freezing the relationships among the records and thus authenticates them at the point at which they become semi-active (see Appendix D, rule A131(q)).

3.2 RETRIEVING RECORDS IN CONTEXT

The profiling of records is designed to make explicit and protect the archival bond between and among records as well as their broader documentary, procedural, provenancial, and juridical-administrative context. It provides one of the necessary conditions not only for creating but also for retrieving records in their appropriate context (registration and classification, which will be discussed in Chapter 4, provide the other necessary conditions). It is not sufficient, however, to guarantee such retrieval. It is necessary, therefore, to develop specific procedures for retrieving records in their appropriate context.

3.2.1. Retrieving records
At the most basic level, retrieving records in context requires that the electronic system (in the case of electronic records) and the records office (in the case of non-electronic records) retrieve the entire record, including all annotations and attachments (see Appendix D, rules A32(c) and (d)). If the record is part of a dossier, the entire dossier must be retrieved along with the record (see Appendix D, rule A32(e)). For electronic records, this entails retrieving, from the repository of records profiles, a view of the profiles of all the other records belonging in the same dossier (see 3.1.2 above). Such procedures are designed to ensure that the officer retrieving the record sees the context of the action in which the requested record participates.

The reason is to ensure that the officer retrieving the record sees the context of the action in which the requested record participates.

3.2.2. Facilitating intellectual access to records
The procedures described above facilitate, primarily, the physical retrieval of records. Other procedures and tools facilitate the intellectual retrieval of records in their appropriate context. These include:

- indexing all the elements contained in the record profile;
- providing a means to search entries in the protocol register;
- building in the capability, within the group and individual spaces of the electronic system, to search records by class code and keyword;
- developing a thesaurus to the classification scheme and linking the thesaural descriptors to the class codes to allow for the searching of records by those descriptors; and
- instituting a procedure for indexing the records using descriptors drawn from the thesaurus (see Appendix D, rule A131(s)).

All of these procedures are concerned with the provision of access points. The terms drawn from the records, the record profile, and the protocol register are examples of uncontrolled, natural language access points or keywords because they are derived from the specific records themselves. The terms drawn from a thesaurus on the other hand are examples of controlled access points because they are drawn from a specialized vocabulary, one that standardizes the scope, meaning and use of the terms included in it.

While natural language access points are useful for locating specific records, they are not particularly helpful in classifying records nor are they particularly effective as a means of locating all relevant records pertaining to an activity or subject. Controlled access points are specifically designed to facilitate efficient and thorough information retrieval. For that reason it is necessary to develop a retrieval system that includes the capacity for searching for records using both uncontrolled and controlled vocabularies.

A thesaurus to the classification scheme is designed to facilitate both the classification and retrieval of records by identifying preferred terms, bringing together non-preferred terms (i.e., synonyms), and noting other relationships, such as broader and narrower terms. The value of a thesaurus lies in its capacity to act as a mediator between an officer and the classification scheme by providing alternate pathways to locate the relevant classification code or retrieve the relevant record(s).[2] An example of a thesaurus to a classification scheme follows[3]:

DISASTER RECOVERY
SN   includes business resumption relating to information technology essential records, and information about previous actions and practices
UF   information technology recovery
recoveries from disasters
BT   DISASTER PREPAREDNESS
NT   BUSINESS RESUMPTION
DISASTER RECOVERY CASE FILES
DISASTER RECOVERY PLANS
RT   DISASTER EVALUATIONS
DISASTER PLANNING
DRILLS (disaster planning)
ESSENTIAL RECORDS

Key to abbreviations:
BT   Broader term
RT   Related term
NT   Narrower term
SN   Scope note
UF   Don't use this term

3.3 CONCLUSION

This chapter has focused on identifying the principal methods for ensuring the creation of electronic records as records, based on the conceptual foundation established in Chapter 1. It has also identified methods that facilitate the retrieval of electronic and non-electronic records in their appropriate contexts. Such methods are designed to ensure that a record is identified explicitly in relation to the action in which it participates from the moment of its creation and that the contexts of its creation and use are protected and preserved throughout its active and semi-active life. The procedures for profiling records and retrieving them in context establish a stable foundation for the integrated management of records in hybrid records systems (i.e., systems containing both electronic and non-electronic records) in general, and for the creation and maintenance of reliable and authentic records within such systems. The following chapter will examine the main methods for ensuring and protecting the reliability and authenticity of records in hybrid records systems.

Chapter 4
Methods for Creating and Maintaining Reliable and Authentic Electronic Records
By Heather MacNeil

The previous chapter focused on identifying the principal methods for creating and retrieving electronic records as records. This chapter focuses on identifying the principal methods for ensuring that such records are created reliable and maintained authentic. The methods draw, implicitly, on the notion of a trusted recordkeeping system, the salient features of which are outlined in the introduction.[1] Because most contemporary records systems are hybrid systems, containing both electronic and non-electronic components, the methods take into account the need to integrate the management of electronic and non-electronic records.

We define a **records system** as the whole of the creator's records and the procedures for creating and maintaining them. These procedures are embodied in the recordkeeping and record-preservation system. The **recordkeeping system** is a set of rules governing the making, receiving, setting aside, and handling of active and semi-active records in the usual and ordinary course of the creator's affairs, and the tools and mechanisms used to implement them. The rules are concerned primarily with ensuring the reliability of records. The **record-preservation system** is a set of rules governing the intellectual and physical maintenance by the creator of semi-active records, and the tools and mechanisms necessary to implement them. These rules are concerned primarily with protecting the authenticity of records. The purpose of the recordkeeping and record-preservation system is to control the creation, handling, and maintenance of all the active and semi-active records of an agency, both electronic and non-electronic.

4.1 ESTABLISHING A FOUNDATION FOR ENSURING THE RELIABILITY AND PROTECTING THE AUTHENTICITY OF THE CREATOR'S RECORDS

Ensuring and protecting the reliability and authenticity of a creator's records begins with establishing certain basic procedural controls over the creation and handling of all its records. Such controls constitute the foundation of the recordkeeping and record-preservation system and include:

4.1.1. establishing and implementing procedures to protect the integrity of the electronic system;
4.1.2. establishing and implementing agency-wide control over all the records in the records system; and
4.1.3. establishing and implementing access privileges.

These basic procedural controls underpin the more specific methods for ensuring reliability and authenticity that will be discussed in sections 4.2 and 4.3 of this chapter.

4.1.1. Establishing and implementing procedures to protect the integrity of the electronic system

Specific procedures to protect the integrity of the electronic component of the records system are necessary because proof of the integrity of the electronic system implies proof of the integrity of the records that are created and/or stored within it.[2] The procedures associated with the protection of the integrity of the electronic system include determining the requirements of the system; establishing procedures for preventing the loss or corruption of the records within the system; and maintaining an audit trail of the system.

Determining the requirements of the electronic system includes identifying (1) functional requirements; (2) national and international documentation and communication standards; (3) the metadata of the electronic system; (4) office applications and communication software to be used to create, handle and preserve records; and (5) interoperability requirements of office applications, communication software, and recordkeeping software (see Appendix D, rule A131(y)).

Preventing the loss or corruption of electronic records due to unauthorized additions, deletions, or alterations includes providing the electronic system with the capability to restrict access to the backup procedures to authorized personnel; prescribing the periodic creation of backup copies of records and their profiles and maintaining a system backup (see Appendix D, rule A131(u)). Preventing the loss of records due to factors such as technological obsolescence involves planning upgrades to the agency's recordkeeping technology base; ensuring the ability to retrieve and use stored records when components of the electronic system are changed; and migrating records (see Appendix D, rule A131(v)). The effectiveness of these procedural controls is verified by maintaining an audit trail of every transmission (date, time, persons, action or matter) within the records system (see Appendix D, rule A131(t)), as well as a specific audit trail of additions and changes to records since the last periodic backup to facilitate the recovery of records in the event of system failure (see Appendix D, rule A131(t) and (u)).

4.1.2. Establishing agency-wide control over all the records in the records system

Agency-wide control over the electronic component of the records system is accomplished by establishing records management domains within the electronic system (see Appendix D, rule A131(c)). These domains define the boundaries of individual space, group space, and general space. **Individual space** corresponds to the jurisdiction of the officer to whom it is assigned by the agency. **Group space** corresponds to the jurisdiction of the office, program, team, committee, working group to which a specific competence, charge, responsibility, or task has been assigned by the agency. **General space** corresponds to the jurisdiction of the records office, which is responsible for the central records system (i.e., the central registry) of the agency. The procedural rules define, on the basis of these domains, the space in which electronic records can be made, received, revised, modified or otherwise altered; the space in which they can be individually destroyed; the space in which they will be classified and registered; the space in which originals are stored; the space in which specific elements of the record profile must be filled in; the space in which the retention schedule is implemented; the right of access to each space; and the way in which electronic records will move inside and outside the agency (see Appendix D, rule A131(d)). Each domain corresponds to an increased level of control, with the least stringent controls being imposed on records residing in the individual space and the most stringent being imposed on records residing in the general space.

The purpose of establishing records management domains within the electronic system is to approximate the level of control associated with traditional central registry systems. In a traditional central registry system exclusive competence for recordkeeping and record-preservation was given to the **records office**. In a hybrid records environment, the records office and **action officers** necessarily share that competence. The creation of records management domains is designed to ensure that electronic records created and used by action officers are subject to controls similar to those traditionally imposed on non-electronic records by a central records office.

Agency-wide control over the non-electronic component of the records system is accomplished by vesting the records office with the exclusive competence for the profiling, classification, registration (when applicable), and consignment to the central records system of all incoming, outgoing, and internal non-electronic records (see Appendix D, rule A131(e) (f)).

4.1.3. Establishing and implementing access privileges
Access privileges refer to the authority granted to officers within an agency to compile, classify, annotate, read, retrieve, transfer, and destroy records.[3].Access privileges are granted on the basis of competence, established in the course of integrating business and documentary procedures, and connected specifically to classes within the classification scheme.

The procedural rules governing the establishment and implementation of access privileges aim to assert the maximum degree of control over records in the records system as the most effective means of ensuring their reliability in the course of their creation and protecting their authenticity in the course of their use and transmission. Accordingly, the rules assign access privileges to specific offices or officers for each class of records on the basis of their competence; permit only the office or officer that creates the records unrestricted access to them; prohibit the modification[4] of records once they have been classified; allow the handling office or officer[5] and the records office to annotate[6] records; allow the records office access to the records for the purpose of classification; and give the records office exclusive authority to access the records for purposes of transfer or destruction (see Appendix D, rule A123).

4.2 SPECIFIC METHODS FOR ENSURING THE RELIABILITY OF RECORDS

As explained in detail in Chapter 2, reliability refers to a record's capacity to stand for the facts to which it speaks and it depends upon two things: the degree of completeness of a record's form and the degree of control exercised over the documentary procedure in the course of which the record is created. **Completeness** refers to the fact that the record possesses all the elements of intellectual form necessary for it to be capable of achieving the purpose for which it was created.[7] Such elements – which include the dates associated with the record, the persons concurring in its formation, the indication of the action or matter, and the classification code – are captured by and large in the record profile (see 3.1 above). The **documentary procedure** refers to the body of rules governing the creation of records.[8] The more standardised and rigorous the procedure, the more reliable the records are presumed to be.

Specific methods associated with record reliability include:

4.2.1.   integrating business and documentary procedures;
4.2.2.   classifying incoming, outgoing, and internal records; and
4.2.3.   registering incoming and outgoing records

4.2.1. Integrating business and documentary procedures
The basic procedural rules of the recordkeeping and record-preservation system establish agency-wide control over the creation and handling of both electronic and non-electronic records. The integration of business processes and documentary procedures strengthens this control by embedding those rules within specific business processes. The rules for integrating business and documentary procedures support the reliability of records by explicitly connecting records to the actions in which they participate and standardising the procedures for creating and managing those records. (see Appendix D, rule A132).

Integrating business and documentary procedures involves, among other things:

- identifying all the business procedures within each agency function;
- decomposing each procedure into its constituent steps;
- determining the actions taken at each step;
- identifying the records that must be made, received, and handled in carrying out the actions;
- specifying the classification code and disposition of the records; and
- establishing the records' level of confidentiality as well as the methods for auditing and authenticating them.

The integration of business and documentary procedures results in a description of the records associated with each phase of each procedure and the specific requirements linked to them in relation to access privileges, classification, registration, authentication, auditing, and so on. The framework established in the integration of business and documentary procedures constitutes an essential foundation for the establishment of automated workflow rules and procedures.

4.2.2. Classifying records

Classification is a means of identifying and organizing all incoming, outgoing, and internal records in relation to the actions in which they participate. Its primary purpose is to place individual records into the aggregates to which they belong, based on the creator's mandate and functions, thereby codifying the status of those records as evidence and memory of actions. The classification code associated with a record establishes a permanent link between that record and the action to which it relates, and between each record and the previous and subsequent one participating in that same action. Classification thus makes explicit the record's archival bond with other records as well as its broader documentary, procedural, and provenancial context; facilitates the retrieval of records in their appropriate context (see 3.2.3 above); and, when integrated with a retention schedule, also facilitates the effective disposition of records (see Appendix D, rule 122).

Classifying records contributes to reliability specifically because the classification code makes a record complete and because classification itself constitutes an important procedural control over the creation of records. It also contributes to authenticity because it is a critical means of identifying a record in context over time and space.

Since a classification scheme is organized on the basis of a records creator's mandate and functions, it is not possible to generalize its scope and content since these will vary from one creator to the next. It is possible, however, to identify the general principles that should guide the organization of any classification scheme and to define its descriptive elements.

4.2.2.1. Organizing principles of a classification scheme.

A classification scheme identifies and names logical, hierarchical classes of records in terms of agency functions, procedures and actions; describes the scope of each class and the arrangement of the records and/or dossiers within it; and expresses those classes in terms of a coding scheme (see Appendix D, rule A121). The classes identified within the scheme should be comprehensive, incorporating both electronic and non-electronic records. The scope of each class should be unambiguous and, to the extent possible, mutually exclusive. The scheme as a whole should be flexible to permit expansion.

The identification and organization of classes within a classification scheme are based on an analysis of the records creator, i.e., its legislative authority or articles of incorporation, mandate or mission, functions, business procedures, and administrative structure and its records, i.e., their nature, purposes and types (see Appendix D, rule A11). If the primary purpose of classification is to make explicit and protect a record's archival bond and context, and facilitate its retrieval in that context, it follows that the hierarchy of classes within a classification scheme should reflect the hierarchy of actions in which the records participate. Accordingly, the classes within the classification scheme should be organized from the general to the specific, i.e., from the broadest functions of the records creator down to the specific actions the records document.

At the broadest functional level, classification schemes should distinguish between records that document common, facilitative functions (i.e., administrative or housekeeping records) and those that document the distinct, substantive functions of an agency or organization (i.e., operational or program records).

Administrative records support housekeeping functions such as the management of personnel, facilities, finances, property and materiel. They also support common management processes, such as committees, agreements, contracts, information services, legal opinions, and other similar functions. In both cases, while such records support the activities of an agency or organization they do not directly document the performance of its mandate or mission.

Operational records are created by an agency in the course of performing the unique, substantive functions that derive from its specific mandate or mission as defined by statute, regulation, or policy.

Standard classification systems such as the ones developed in the Canadian provincial governments of British Columbia and Nova Scotia are divided along administrative and operational functions. The administrative records of the Government of British Columbia are classified in accordance with the Administrative Records Classification System (ARCS). The operational records of each agency of the Government of British Columbia are classified in accordance with the Operational Records Classification System (ORCS) developed by and for each agency to meet its particular operational needs. A similar distinction is made in the Standard for Administrative Records (STAR) and the Standard for Operational Records (STOR) developed for the classification of the records of the Government of Nova Scotia and its agencies.

Most standard classification systems (including ARCS and ORCS and STAR and STOR) are block-numeric records classification systems, meaning they are based on the assignment of blocks of numbers to represent the main groups, primaries and secondaries.

4.2.2.2. Descriptive elements in the classification scheme.[9] The following are the essential descriptive elements to be included in any classification scheme:

- Main Groups or Sections
- Primaries
- Explanatory Notes and Cross-References
- Secondaries
- Classification Code

Main Groups or Sections.[10] The main groups or sections within any classification scheme correspond to the overall functions of an agency. In an administrative classification scheme, the main groups or sections represent the basic administrative or facilitative functions of any records creator. For example, in STAR, the main groups are:

- Administration
- Facilities management
- Financial management
- Human resources management
- Information management
- Materiel management

While the administrative functions of a records creator tend to be generic, its operational functions are unique and therefore the number and nature of the main groups will vary from one creator to the next. For example, in the ORCS of the B.C. Ministry of Children and Families the main groups correspond to the main substantive functions of the ministry, i.e.:

- Adoption
- Education, training, and employment
- Family and personal support services
- Residential and non-residential resources
- Services to support community development

Primaries. Each main group is subdivided into primaries, each of which pertains to a function, activity, or subject within the main group. For example, in STAR, the main group Administration is subdivided into the following primaries:

- Administration—General
- Accidents
- Campaigns and Canvassing
- Ceremonies and Visits
- Communications Management
- Corporations, Companies, and Firms
- Disaster Preparedness and Recovery
- Information Services—General
- Information Services—Advertising
- Information Services—Media Relations
- Information Services—Public Relations
- Information Services—Publishing (Should these be bulleted also?)
- Risk Management
- Support Services—General
- Support Services—Hospitality
- Support Services—Photocopying
- Support Services—Postal

- Support Services—Secretarial

Within a main group or section, primaries may be grouped into related clusters or *primary blocks*. In STAR, primary blocks are defined are "clusters of two or more related primaries that share a function title." In the example above, "Information Services" and "Support Services" constitute primary blocks.

Explanatory Notes and Cross-References. Explanatory notes clarify and elaborate on the scope and content of a class and are normally included at the main group and primary levels. In certain cases, they may also be provided at the level of secondaries. Such notes may be accompanied by cross-references that direct the user to other relevant classes. For example, the following explanatory note and cross-references are given for the primary "Disaster Preparedness and Recovery" within the Administration main group.

> 1000-1999 ADMINISTRATION
> 1200 Disaster Preparedness and Recovery
> Used for disaster preparedness, emergency measures, and business resumption following all disasters causing accidental or purposeful loss or disruption of business operations. Covers plans to protect human life and safety during a disaster. Contains evaluation of potential disasters, disaster response and business resumption plans, tests and drills, and recovery activities. Also includes business resumption relating to information technology and essential records, and information about previous action plans, fire evacuation plans, and practices. Examples: disaster preparedness plans, disaster response plans, disaster recovery plans, fire evacuation plans, recovery case files.
> For accidents see 1050, Administration, Accidents
> For active, archival, or destroyed records see 5650, Information Management, Records Management—Description and Records Scheduling
> For contingency planning see 2650, Facilities Management, Physical Security
> For health and safety in the workplace see 4500 see 4500, Human Resources Management, Occupational Health and Safety
> For information security see 5250, Information Management, Information Security
> For risk assessment see 1700, Administration, Risk Assessment
> For systems backup and protection of information see 5250, Information Management, Information Security

Secondaries. Each primary is subdivided into secondaries. Secondaries designate specific groupings of records relating to the function covered by the primary. Most classification schemes identify three distinct types of secondaries: standardized, subject, and case file secondaries.

a) *Standardized Secondaries*. Standardized secondaries are a list of secondaries which is included in all primaries and is common to both administrative and operational records classification schemes. In STAR the standardized list is called the *common menu*; in ARCS and ORCS, it is called the *reserved secondaries*.

There are only two reserved secondaries of the ARCS and ORCS:

-00   Policy and procedures
-01   General.

The STAR common menu is considerably more detailed and includes the following secondaries:

-00   Policies, Procedures, and Standards
-01   General
-02   Acts and Legislation
-03   Associations and Conferences
-04   Committees
-05   Contracts and Agreements
-06   Legal Matters
-07   Planning and Review
-08   Reports and Statistics

b) *Subject File Secondaries.* Subject file secondaries are reserved for subject files, i.e., files that contain information about specific topics, functions, or activities and that are organized according to their general information content. In STAR, -20 is reserved in all primaries as a common secondary title for subject files. For example:

ADMINISTRATION
1200 Disaster Preparedness and Recovery
        -20 Subject files
        -21 Test drills
        -22 Essential Records Lists
        -23 Fire Evacuation Plans
        -24 Disaster Preparedness, Response, and Recovery Plans

c) *Case File Secondaries.* Case files pertain to a specific, time-limited entity such as an event, project, business action, transaction, product, organizations, or individual. Case file secondaries are usually subdivided through the use of codes that identify the specific person, event, project, or other entity covered by the files. For example:

1200 Disaster Preparedness and Recovery
        -30   Disaster Recovery Case Files
                Fi-821/Shelburne Fire
                Fl-33/Truro Flood

Classification Code. Each class within a classification scheme has a unique numerical or alphabetical symbol assigned to it, i.e., a classification code. When attached to a record, the classification code uniquely identifies and locates that record in relation to the specific class and, when applicable, the specific dossier to which it belongs (see Appendix D, rule A23).

According to the procedural rules we have established, the classification code is attached to the record by recording it on the record profile form. The classification code is a three-part notation that incorporates the following elements:

- **class code**, i.e., the combined primary and secondary code of the class in which the record belongs, as it appears in the classification scheme;

- **dossier identifier**, i.e., the identifier for the dossier in which the record belongs. It may be constituted by the name of a person or organization, a symbol, a progressive number, a date, or a specific topic within the class's general subject; and

- **record item identifier**, i.e, the progressive number of the record within the dossier (or, in the absence of dossiers, within the specific class). This identifier is assigned to the record when it is consigned to the central records system.

4.2.3. Registering incoming and outgoing records
The registration of all incoming and outgoing records is another means of demonstrating interrelationships among records and making explicit the archival bond between and among them. During the middle ages, registration was an important aspect of papal and royal chancery procedures. It involved the copying of important outgoing documents into a book called a register. Registers served as memory of acts and decisions taken and could be referred to if necessary to check precedents and to establish the authenticity of documents issued by chanceries. Over time, the complete transcription of the record was gradually replaced by the selective recording of key identifying elements drawn from the protocol (top portion) of the record.

In contemporary recordkeeping, registration is still an important means for records creators to establish the authenticity of all incoming and outgoing records. Registration serves the interests of administrative accountability by furnishing evidence of the existence of each record that enters and exits an agency. In fact, in civil law jurisdictions such as Italy, "the protocol register maintained by a public office, which certifies the date of sending or receipt of private or governmental acts, has the nature of a *public act*."[11] Registration serves not only administrative accountability but, also, historical accountability over time because the protocol register preserves evidence of the existence of records and the act to which they relate even after the records themselves no longer exist. The evidence persists in the form of the protocol register entry. This explains why the permanent retention of protocol registers is mandated in many civil law jurisdictions.

Registration is associated with reliability specifically because the protocol number contributes to the completeness of incoming and outgoing records and because registration itself constitutes a rigorous procedural control over the creation of records. It also contributes to authenticity because it provides a circumstantial assurance of a record's genuineness (as it did in medieval times). The authenticity of an incoming or outgoing record may be verified by checking the protocol register.

The procedure of registration consists of assigning to each incoming and outgoing record a unique consecutive number (called a *protocol number*); recording that number in the applicable field of the record profile; and making an entry in the protocol register (see Appendix D, rule A24). The entry records the following information:

- the date the record was received or sent,
- the name of its author and addressee,
- the action or matter to which it relates,
- the classification code, and
- any other information necessary to uniquely identify the record and the action with which it is associated.

To be effective as an accountability tool, a new protocol register should be opened each year and span one calendar or fiscal year (see Appendix D, rules A131(l), A35 (g)).

The information recorded in the protocol register, with the exception of the protocol number and the date received or sent, may be extracted from the record profile (see Appendix D, rule A131(l)). This implies that, when records are removed or destroyed, along with their profile, the information will continue to exist as a protocol register entry for as long as the protocol register is retained.

4.3 PROTECTING AUTHENTICITY

A document is authentic if it can be demonstrated that it is what it claims to be and has not been corrupted or tampered with since its creation. It is linked to the record's state, mode and form of transmission, and to the manner of its preservation and custody.[12] While the basic procedural controls described in section 4.1 above support the protection of the authenticity of a creator's records, we have identified a number of additional methods that aim specifically at:

4.3.1.   controlling the handling and use of records;
4.3.2.   controlling the transmission of records; and
4.3.3.   managing the scheduling and disposition of records.

4.3.1. Controlling the handling and use of records
Controlling the handling and use of records involves implementing procedural controls over the retrieval and annotation of records, and establishing specific procedures to protect the confidentiality of records.

4.3.1.1. Controlling retrieval of active and semi-active records. With respect to the retrieval of active records, the records office is responsible for retrieving non-electronic records from the central records system. Before retrieving any non-electronic record, the records office will first verify that the requester's access privileges include permission to view the record (see Appendix D, rule A32(a)). Officers may retrieve electronic records directly from the electronic system on the basis of their access privileges (see Appendix D, rule A131(d) and rule A32(b)).

The records office also has exclusive competence for managing the records in the semi-active storage location and for retrieving them from and returning them to that location (see Appendix D, rule A41).

4.3.1.2. Opening dossiers. A repertory of dossiers is a finding aid, maintained within the electronic system, the purpose of which is to identify and keep track of each dossier that has been opened within each class in the classification scheme. The repertory is an essential tool because it documents the creation and existence of all dossiers. In this respect, the repertory not only supports the retrieval and control of dossiers, it also provides evidence of their authenticity. A typical entry in the repertory includes the name of the dossier, the names of its subdossiers (if applicable), and its routing through administrative offices during its life cycle (see Appendix D, rule A23).

4.3.1.3. Establishing and implementing a tracking and location system for non-electronic records. A tracking and location system is a set of rules aimed at exercising physical and administrative control over the movement and storage of active and semi-active records (see Appendix D, rule A131(r)). The records office is competent for maintaining the system. Its responsibilities include:

- instituting charge out procedures for all the records preservation units (e.g., folders, volumes, tapes, disks) which are not contained within the electronic system;
- when a closed dossier is removed from the system, assigning a location which is recorded within the electronic system according to class; and
- establishing a procedure for maintaining up-to-date location information for all active and semi-active records in all media.

4.3.1.4. Controlling annotations. With respect to annotating records, the procedural rules stipulate, among other things, that each annotation be signed and dated and that the annotation be inextricably bound to the record. Only the office or officer competent for the action in which the record participates is permitted to annotate a record in connection to the execution and/or handling of the action or matter; and only the records office is permitted to annotate a record for records management purposes (see Appendix D, rule A34).

4.3.1.5. Protecting confidentiality. In addition to defining and implementing access privileges, it is necessary to establish procedures for protecting the confidentiality of records (see Appendix D, rule A131(o)). The procedural rules should aim at:

- identifying confidential classes of records;
- identifying the method for protecting confidentiality for every record medium;
- assigning responsibility for implementing the methods and rules; and
- identifying methods of ensuring confidentiality of transmissions within and outside the agency.

4.3.2. Controlling the transmission of records
Controlling the transmission of records involves establishing the status of records as originals, drafts, or copies, standardizing the degree of authority that will be accorded to records, and centralizing the authority for making authentic copies of records.

4.3.2.1. Establishing state of transmission and draft control. The state of transmission of a record refers to its degree of development and authority when it is set aside; in other words, its status as a *draft, copy,* or *original*. A *draft* is a temporary compilation of a document intended for correction; drafts may be in various stages of completion. A *copy* is a reproduction of a record made either from an original, a draft or another copy. An *original* is the first complete and effective record. An original record is one that is complete (i.e., its form is the one intended by its author and/or required by the juridical system), primitive (i.e., it is the first to be produced in its complete form), and effective (i.e., it is capable of reaching the effects for which it was produced).

The state of transmission of electronic records specifically is assessed in relation to its routing in the electronic system (see Appendix D, rule A131(m)). Several examples serve to illustrate this. A record that has not been transmitted is a draft. A record transmitted to the general space is received as an original. A record transmitted externally is consigned to the central record system of the sender as a copy of the last draft and received by the addressee as an original. A record received in the group space is received as an original but can be altered and transformed into a draft of another record, and so on.

Draft control is maintained by sequentially numbering the various drafts of the same record circulating in the group and individual spaces. The draft number is recorded in the record profile as an annotation. In addition, every comment on drafts received in the group space is an original and must be capable of being linked to the draft to which it relates.

4.3.2.2. Controlling copies. To copy records means to make a reproduction of a record in any state of transmission for business purposes. In the rules identified for controlling copies, the records office is given exclusive competence for the following activities:

- copying non-electronic records stored in the central records system;
- making authentic copies of the records in the central records system; and

- routinely copying records for preservation or security reasons, or for satisfying external requests.

The procedural rules also identify the various types of copies (e.g., simple, imitative, copy in the form of original, and authentic[13]) that the electronic system (in the case of electronic records) or the records office (in the case of non-electronic records) will produce (see Appendix D, rule A131(p)). They also establish the degree of authority to be accorded to each type (see Appendix D, rule A33). For example, the rules stipulate that a simple copy cannot be used as an authoritative or authentic copy; that an authentic copy is required to satisfy external requests for records; and that an imitative authentic copy is the only type of copy used for preservation purposes.

4.3.3. Managing the retention and final disposition of records

The scheduling and regular disposition of records are methods of identifying and preserving records possessing long-term or permanent value and of identifying and destroying in a timely fashion records possessing limited, short-term value. A comprehensive records schedule accompanied by procedures for its implementation is an essential means by which a records creator accounts for the presence or absence of records within the records system at any given time. The proper management of records retention and disposition strengthens the reliability and authenticity of the records system as a whole. It serves the interests of authenticity specifically because it constitutes an essential procedural control over the preservation and custody of active and semi-active records and provides justification for records destruction.

4.3.3.1. Creating a retention schedule. A retention schedule is a timetable associated with each class of record that determines its period of active, and semi-active retention, establishes the office of primary responsibility and indicates the final disposition of the records (either destruction or transfer to a competent archival body) (see Appendix D, rule A122). In standard classification systems such as ARCS and ORCS and STAR and STOR, and as we recommend, the retention schedule is integrated with the classification scheme through the linking of its components to primary and/or secondary classes within that scheme.

The essential components of a records schedule are:

- Retention Period
- Medium of Retention
- Final Disposition
- Designation of Office of Primary Responsibility

Retention Period. The retention period for a given class of records within the classification scheme is determined on the basis of the creator's administrative, legal, fiscal, and audit needs for the records belonging to that class. Knowledge of those needs in turn derives from information about the records creator, its business procedures and its records, and it may be found in a variety of sources, among them statutes, regulations, procedural manuals, the records inventory, and the classification scheme.

The active retention period for a class of records is based on the length of time the records within that class are needed for carrying out the actions for which they were created. The semi-active retention period for a class of records is based on the length of time the records within that class are needed by the creator for reference purposes. In an integrated classification scheme and retention schedule, the retention periods are listed in columns beside the classes to which they refer.

Medium of Retention. In addition to identifying the retention periods for classes of records, the retention schedule should identify the medium on which semi-active records will be retained. The identification of the medium for retention is based on a number of factors, among them: *frequency of use* (i.e., the number of times within a determined time span that a record needs to be retrieved for use by the competent office/officer), *location of use* (i.e., the place(s) where a given type of record needs to be consulted), *reference time* (i.e., the amount of uninterrupted time the competent office/officer needs to consult a given type of record), and *retrieval time* (i.e., the amount of time it takes to retrieve the specific record required by the competent office/officer).

Final Disposition. The final disposition of a class of records is determined on the basis of the continuing value of the records to the creator and to society at large as evidence and memory of the creator and its activities. If, on the one hand, it is determined that records belonging to a given class of records have no further value once they are no longer needed to carry out actions or for reference purposes, the final disposition of the records is destruction. If, on the other hand, it is determined that the records in a given class have continuing value, the final disposition of all or part of those records is transfer to a competent archival body for long-term preservation. In an integrated classification scheme and retention schedule, two kinds of permanent retention are identified: full retention, when all the records are to be preserved and selective retention, when only a portion of the records is to be preserved.

Office of Primary Responsibility. The Office of Primary Responsibility is the office given the formal competence for maintaining the original (or official) records belonging to a given class within the integrated classification scheme and retention schedule. The purpose of designating an Office of Primary Responsibility for each class of record is to reduce duplication and to designate accountability for records. Offices other than the Office of Primary Responsibility that maintain copies of records have distinct retention periods.

4.3.3.2. Implementing the records schedule. Implementing the terms of the records schedule involves establishing procedures for removing records from the central records system when they are no longer active, reviewing and converting records in semi-active storage, and disposing of the records when they become inactive, either by destroying inactive records or transferring custody of them to a competent archival body.

In our view, competence for carrying out all these activities is shared by the records office and the Office of Primary Responsibility. Although the records office is directly responsible for removing records from the central records system, transferring them to archival custody, or destroying them, it must obtain authorization to do so from the Office of Primary Responsibility.

Removing Records from the Central Records System. When records are no longer active, the records office must ensure that records are removed from the central records system and transferred, either to semi-active storage or to a competent archival body, The profiles of these records, along with any finding aids and supporting documentation, e.g., indexes, data directories, data dictionaries, should be removed and transferred at the same time.

For incoming and outgoing records, the corresponding entry in the protocol register (see 4.2.3 above) is not removed from the central records system. The retention and disposition of individual protocol register entries entirely depends on the retention and disposition established for the protocol register as a whole.

Before they are removed from the central records system, a final view should be created of the record profiles of all the records in each dossier or, when the class does not contain dossiers, a final view of the profiles of all the records in the class for each year. The creation of a final view is a way of freezing the relationships among the records and thus serves the purpose of authenticating them at the point at which they are transferred either to semi-active storage or to a competent archival body. One copy of the final view will remain in the general space of the electronic system while the other copy accompanies the dossier. In the case of non-electronic records, the profiles for each dossier will be printed out and attached to the dossier (see Appendix D, rule A131(n), (q), (w)).

In addition, an annotation should be added to all the record profiles indicating the medium on which the records are being transferred and the date of removal (see Appendix D, rule A35).

Reviewing Semi-Active Records. Regular review of semi-active records by the records office is necessary to determine whether the records need to be converted or maintained as they are, and whether they have reached the end of their semi-active period and therefore are ready to be transferred to a competent archival body or destroyed. If the records office determines that the reviewed records need to be converted, then it has the authority to determine the medium and physical form of the records (see Appendix D, rule A42).

Converting Semi-Active Records. Converting semi-active records means changing the record's medium and/or physical form of a record in the usual and ordinary course of business, leaving intact its intellectual form. Exclusive competence for converting records is given to the records office, which must ensure that conversion does not compromise the records' authenticity. The procedures for converting records include disposing of source records after conversion, providing quality control assurances, and authenticating each form of conversion. One method of authenticating the conversion is to annotate the record profile with an indication of the new medium and physical form, along with the date of conversion (see Appendix D, rule A43).

Destroying Inactive Records. Once the records office has obtained authorization from the Office of Primary Responsibility to destroy records, its essential tasks are to determine the appropriate method of destruction, depending on the medium and degree of sensitivity of the records; and to ensure that when dossiers are destroyed, the final views of their profiles which have remained in the central records system will be destroyed along with them. (rule Appendix D, rule A43)

Transferring Custody of Inactive Records. Once authority to transfer records has been obtained from the Office of Primary Responsibility the records office has two final tasks, which are designed to provide a final authentication of the records (see Appendix D, rule A44). The first task is to create a final view of the dossiers' profiles, including a final annotation indicating the date of transfer that will accompany the dossiers as an electronic file in the case of electronic records and as a printout in the case of non-electronic records. This final view serves to authenticate those dossiers at the point of transfer to the archival body. Its second task is to ensure that the final view of the dossiers, which may have been annotated during the records' semi-active period, is removed from the agency's records system, along with the dossiers.

4.4   ENSURING   THE   CONTINUING   EFFECTIVENESS   OF   THE RECORDKEEPING AND RECORD-PRESERVATION SYSTEM

4.4.1. Codification and training
If the procedural rules of the recordkeeping and record-preservation system are to be effective, it is essential that the rules be written down in a procedures manual so that every officer within the agency may learn or refer to them. A comprehensive and systematic training program aimed at all agency personnel is a necessary corollary to such codification. Both codification and training are essential not only to ensure consistency in the implementation of the rules but also to support an inference of record reliability and authenticity in the event of a legal dispute.

4.4.2. Ongoing monitoring and upgrading
Finally, the procedural rules for recordkeeping and record preservation need to be monitored and upgraded in response to changes in the **juridical system**, changes in policies or procedures, changes in technology, and so on (see Appendix D, rules A141, A142, and A143). This phase of the process of records management includes:

- monitoring the records system to determine officer compliance with th
  procedural rules;
- evaluating the adequacy of system backup and recovery procedures;
- identifying changes in legal context, business procedures, classes of records
  and office of primary responsibility for classes of records;
- determining changes in retention requirements for existing classes
  records, and
- modifying the procedural rules accordingly.

4.5 CONCLUSION

This chapter has focused on identifying general and specific methods fo
ensuring and protecting the reliability and authenticity of electronic records base
on the conceptual foundation established in Chapter 2. The methods embody th
principal features of a trusted recordkeeping and record-preservation system fo
active and semi-active records and are predicated on the existence of hybri
records systems that contain both electronic and non-electronic records.

Conclusion

Since the research on this project began, several
guide software developers and organizations to
effective management of records. In one insta
development of a standard. It is in line with many o

In the first case, the United States Department of
our work to produce a standard to certify re
software for use by branches and offices of the
National Archives and Records Administration
known as *Standard for Electronic Records M*
(DoD 5015.2-STD), for use by federal agencie:
adopt all of the recommendations we make b
of how the results of our work can be scale
juridical, organizational, and administrative cir

The requirements set out in our work can b
standards: the International Standards Org
Standard on Records Management[2] and the
Requirements Specification (MoReq).[3] L:
standards pay considerable attention to th
records management. Indeed, the MoReq
on functional requirements for the manage

As salutary as it is that good advice i:
records management software, much els
each entity responsible to manage its re
needs to put in place a coherent regime
just records managers but also a
recordkeeping in the new office
technology. Beyond that, as archival e
mention the need to provide future ar
understanding of both the theory an
records-preservation in the electron
glibly of the paperless office, when i
it. Since then, networks, includin
communicate all manner of electro
manage those documents as relia
memorials of the actions they expr
arrive, understanding of what nee
organizational behavior. We hope
form will assist that process, for tl
and more complex records, crea
form.

ordinary course of business, leaving intact its intellectual form. Exclusive competence for converting records is given to the records office, which must ensure that conversion does not compromise the records' authenticity. The procedures for converting records include disposing of source records after conversion, providing quality control assurances, and authenticating each form of conversion. One method of authenticating the conversion is to annotate the record profile with an indication of the new medium and physical form, along with the date of conversion (see Appendix D, rule A43).

Destroying Inactive Records. Once the records office has obtained authorization from the Office of Primary Responsibility to destroy records, its essential tasks are to determine the appropriate method of destruction, depending on the medium and degree of sensitivity of the records; and to ensure that when dossiers are destroyed, the final views of their profiles which have remained in the central records system will be destroyed along with them. (rule Appendix D, rule A43)

Transferring Custody of Inactive Records. Once authority to transfer records has been obtained from the Office of Primary Responsibility the records office has two final tasks, which are designed to provide a final authentication of the records (see Appendix D, rule A44). The first task is to create a final view of the dossiers' profiles, including a final annotation indicating the date of transfer that will accompany the dossiers as an electronic file in the case of electronic records and as a printout in the case of non-electronic records. This final view serves to authenticate those dossiers at the point of transfer to the archival body. Its second task is to ensure that the final view of the dossiers, which may have been annotated during the records' semi-active period, is removed from the agency's records system, along with the dossiers.

4.4 ENSURING THE CONTINUING EFFECTIVENESS OF THE RECORDKEEPING AND RECORD-PRESERVATION SYSTEM

4.4.1. Codification and training
If the procedural rules of the recordkeeping and record-preservation system are to be effective, it is essential that the rules be written down in a procedures manual so that every officer within the agency may learn or refer to them. A comprehensive and systematic training program aimed at all agency personnel is a necessary corollary to such codification. Both codification and training are essential not only to ensure consistency in the implementation of the rules but also to support an inference of record reliability and authenticity in the event of a legal dispute.

4.4.2. Ongoing monitoring and upgrading
Finally, the procedural rules for recordkeeping and record preservation need to be monitored and upgraded in response to changes in the **juridical system**, changes in policies or procedures, changes in technology, and so on (see Appendix D, rules A141, A142, and A143). This phase of the process of records management includes:

- monitoring the records system to determine officer compliance with the procedural rules;
- evaluating the adequacy of system backup and recovery procedures;
- identifying changes in legal context, business procedures, classes of records, and office of primary responsibility for classes of records;
- determining changes in retention requirements for existing classes of records, and
- modifying the procedural rules accordingly.

4.5 CONCLUSION

This chapter has focused on identifying general and specific methods for ensuring and protecting the reliability and authenticity of electronic records based on the conceptual foundation established in Chapter 2. The methods embody the principal features of a trusted recordkeeping and record-preservation system for active and semi-active records and are predicated on the existence of hybrid records systems that contain both electronic and non-electronic records.

Conclusion

Since the research on this project began, several standards have appeared to guide software developers and organizations to meet the requirements for effective management of records. In one instance, our work influenced the development of a standard. It is in line with many of the features of two others.

In the first case, the United States Department of Defense adapted the results of our work to produce a standard to certify records management application software for use by branches and offices of the Department. The United States National Archives and Records Administration has also endorsed this standard, known as *Standard for Electronic Records Management Software Applications* (DoD 5015.2-STD), for use by federal agencies.[1] Although DoD 5015.2 does not adopt all of the recommendations we make by any means, it is a good example of how the results of our work can be scaled and adapted to suit a particular juridical, organizational, and administrative circumstance.

The requirements set out in our work can be compared with those in two other standards: the International Standards Organization's (ISO) *Draft International Standard on Records Management*[2] and the European Commission's (EC) *Model Requirements Specification* (MoReq).[3] Like the DoD standard, both these standards pay considerable attention to the required software functionalities for records management. Indeed, the MoReq standard states that it "focuses mainly on functional requirements for the management of electronic records."[4]

As salutary as it is that good advice is available to developers of electronic records management software, much else needs to be done. As our work shows, each entity responsible to manage its records, both electronic and non-electronic, needs to put in place a coherent regime of policies and procedures and train not just records managers but also action officers in the requirements for recordkeeping in the new office environment dominated by information technology. Beyond that, as archival educators, we would be remiss if we did not mention the need to provide future archivists and records managers with a deep understanding of both the theory and methods of effective recordkeeping and records-preservation in the electronic environment. Years ago, people talked glibly of the paperless office, when in fact the technology was not up to realizing it. Since then, networks, including the Internet, have made it possible to communicate all manner of electronic documents. It is still a great challenge to manage those documents as reliable records and preserve them as authentic memorials of the actions they express. Although the paperless office may never arrive, understanding of what needs to be done is slowly making its way into organizational behavior. We hope that the wider availability of our work in this form will assist that process, for the future is very likely to bring us more records, and more complex records, created and maintained exclusively in the electronic form.

Notes

Introduction

[1] United Nations, Advisory Committee for the Co-ordination of Information Systems (ACCIS), *Management of Electronic Records: Issues and Guidelines* (New York: United Nations, 1990), 28. Hereinafter cited as ACCIS report.

[2] ACCIS report, 29.

[3] ACCIS report, 30.

[4] ACCIS report, 32-34.

[5] John McDonald, "Managing Records in the Modern Office: Taming the Wild Frontier," *Archivaria* 39 (Spring 1995): 70-71.

[6] Margaret Hedstrom, "Building Records Keeping Systems: Archivists Are Not Alone on the Wild Frontier," *Archivaria* 44 (Fall 1997): 57.

[7] For a detailed analysis of the case, see Heather MacNeil, *Trusting Records: Legal, Historical and Diplomatic Perspectives* (Dordrecht: Kluwer Academic Publishers, 2000), 77-85. For a perspective on the broader archival issues raised by the case, see David Bearman, "The Implications of *Armstrong v. Executive Office of the President* for Archival Management of Electronic Records," *The American Archivist* 56 (Fall 1993): 674-689. For a contemporary statement by the Society of American Archivists on the issues, see "Archival Issues Raised by Information Stored in Electronic Form," *Archival Outlook* (May 1995): 8-9.

[8] The first article was Luciana Duranti and Terry Eastwood, "Protecting Electronic Evidence: A Progress Report on a Research Study and its Methodology," *Archivi & Computer* 3 (1995): 213-50. A list of all the articles related to the research is in Appendix F.

[9] For a discussion of deductive versus inductive methods of research in archival science, see Terry Eastwood, "What is Archival Theory and Why Is It Important?," *Archivaria* 37 (Spring 1994): 122-30. For discussion and comparison of our work with other research on electronic records-keeping, see Hedstrom, "Building Records Keeping Systems," 46-56, and Paul Marsden, "When is the Future? Comparative Notes on the Electronic Record-Keeping Projects of the University of Pittsburgh and the University of British Columbia," *Archivaria* (Spring 1997): 158-73.

[10] Alan Kowlowitz, "Appraising in a vacuum: Electronic Records Appraisal Issues—A View From the Trenches," in "Archival Management of Electronic Records," ed. David Bearman, *Archives and Museum Informatics Technical Report No 13* (1991): 31.

Chapter One

[1] These hypotheses were articulated in templates, against which specific documentary manifestations could be compared for the purpose of drawing conclusions on their nature by analogy. For a full explanation of the templates, see Luciana Duranti and Terry Eastwood, "Protecting Electronic Evidence: A Progress Report," *Archivi & Computer* 5:3 (1995): 222-232. The templates are reproduced in Appendix A.

[2] The fact that "archival document" is the diplomatic term for "record" explains the use of the term by certain British authors, like Jenkinson, who defines an archival document as "one which is drawn up or used in the course of an administrative or executive transaction (whether public or private) of which itself formed a part; and subsequently preserved in their own custody for their own information by the person or persons responsible for that transaction and their legitimate successors." Hilary Jenkinson, *A Manual of Archive Administration* (Oxford: Clarendon Press, 1922), 11.

[3] Cesare Paoli, *Diplomatica*, 2nd ed. (Firenze: Sansoni, 1942). For a discussion of the diplomatic definitions of document see Luciana Duranti, "Diplomatics: New Uses for an Old Science," *Archivaria* 28 (Summer 1989): 15-16. The series of articles of which this is the were published in a book. Luciana Duranti, *Diplomatics: New Uses for an Old Science* (Lanham, MD: The Scarecrow Press, 1998).

[4] A juridical system is a social group organized on the basis of a system of rules that the group recognizes as binding. See Luciana Duranti, "Diplomatics: New Uses for an Old Science (Part II)" *Archivaria* 29 (Winter 1989-90): 5.

[5] This relationship can be found in a written document, but, in common law countries, only if such document is admissible in court under relevancy and exclusionary rules of evidence. The exclusionary rules include a preferential rule (the best evidence rule), the analytic rules (those comprising the hearsay rules), and a sufficiency rule (the authentication rule). In civil law countries, the relationship exists only if the document is directly relevant to the case. In both juridical systems, the concept of evidence is at one time much broader than that of record--as it encompasses oral

testimony, material evidence, and written documents that are not generated in the course of business--and much more specific, as it requires a specific relationship.

[6] Records can be considered "facts" themselves: visible facts at which records makers are present. See Luciana Duranti, "Diplomatics: New Uses for an Old Science (Part II)": 11.

[7] Dom Jean Mabillon, *De re diplomatica libri VI* (Paris, 1681)

[8] Lester K. Born, "Baldassarre Bonifacio and His Essay 'De Archivis'," *The American Archivist* 4 (1941): 221-237.

[9] In many evidence acts, the admissibility of business records is not only restricted to those which have been created in the usual and ordinary course of business, but there is the additional requirement that it be the usual and ordinary course of business to create such records. This criterion is introduced as a disincentive to businesses that might be tempted to introduce self-serving evidence that does not form part of the fulfilment of the business duty, but is simply made in relation to it.

[10] When acts, persons, and procedures manifest themselves "formally" in an archival document, they constitute its **content**, what the document is about.

[11] See for example Hilary Jenkinson, *A Manual of Archival Administration* (Percy, Lund, Humphries, and Co.: London, 1937), p. 97 et seq.; Giorgio Cencetti, "Il fondamento teorico della dottrina archivistica," *Archivi* II, VI (1939): 40; and Elio Lodolini, *Archivistica. Principi e Problemi*, 6th edition (Franco Angeli: Milano, 1992), 132 and 149. See also Elio Lodolini, "The War of Independence of Archivists," *Archivaria* 28 (Summer 1989): 38, 41.

[12] As will be seen later, according to archival science, a record is created when, after being made or received, it is set aside by including it in the whole body of records--or archival fonds--of the physical or juridical person who made or received it for action or reference.

[13] The archival concept of archival bond has also guided the research team to reject the definition of records as "recorded transactions," which has become popular among some archival commentators. This trend began in 1989, with the definition found in ASSIS Report (cited in n. 1, Introduction), 10. The primary reason for the rejection is that, besides determining the structure of the archival body of records, the archival bond is the primary identifying component of each record, as several identical documents become as many distinct records after they acquire the archival bond. Because the archival bond is what transforms a document into a record, one cannot say that records are "recorded transactions." Documents that are expression of a transaction are not records until they are put into relation with other records, while documents that are not expression of a transaction become records at the moment when they acquire an archival bond with other documents participating in the same activity. Undoubtedly, before making such statement, one should first define what a transaction is. According to diplomatics, a transaction is a special type of act that aims to change the relationships between two or more parties. Diplomatically, transactions are embodied in records whose written form is required by law for an act to exist or to be proven, but they may only incidentally relate to all records whose written form is not required by law. Legally, a transaction is "an act or agreement, or several acts or agreements having some connection with each other, in which more than one person is concerned, and by which the legal relations of such persons between themselves are altered." (*Black's Law Dictionary*, 5th edition, "transaction"). Thus, by saying that records are recorded transactions, one eliminates from the records category every document that is not produced as a legal requirement and in a complete and reliable form. If one instead uses the term transaction in the computer science meaning of electronic communication, then one includes in the records category anything that crosses electronic boundaries. Archival science and diplomatics do not require completeness and reliability for a record to exist, neither do they require that it be *made* in the course of business. Rather, they require that a record be *created* in the course of business, and creation occurs at the arising of the archival bond.

[14] Data, or better a datum, is taken to be the smallest meaningful fact.

[15] For an ample discussion on the definition of information, see Trevor Livelton, *Archival Theory, Records, and the Public* (Lanham, Md. & London: The Society of American Archivists and The Scarecrow Press, Inc., 1996), 61-63. As Livelton notes, Samuel Johnson defined information as "intelligence given," conveying the same concept of a message meant for communication as that presented here.

[16] The expression used by the research team to denote the idea of retention is "set aside."

[17] These definitions have been developed from diplomatics by the research team for the purposes of this research project.

[18] See Luciana Duranti, "Diplomatics: New Uses for an Old Science," *Archivaria* 28 (Summer 1989): 15, and "Diplomatics: New Uses for an Old Science (Part V)," *Archivaria* 32 (Summer 1991): 6-24.

[19] Special signs are drawings, stamps, symbols indicating the existence of attachments or comments, mottoes, crests, insigna or emblems, signa manus, etc.

[20] See Luciana Duranti, "Diplomatics: New Uses for an Old Science (Part V):" 11-16.

[21] See Heather MacNeil, "Metadata Strategies and Archival Description: Comparing Apples to Oranges," *Archivaria* 39 (Spring 1995): 22-32.

[22] The term person comes from the Latin *persona*, meaning mask, role, or character.

[23] Physical or juridical persons can be public or private. Public persons are persons having jurisdiction over matters related to or affecting the whole people of a nation, state or community, that is, they are persons invested with some measure of sovereignty. Private persons are persons who do not have jurisdiction in public matters.

[24] It has to be pointed out that the writer cannot be a record office or secretary who, lacking the authority to sign, are not considered to be persons in the context of records creation. A comprehensive discussion of persons from a diplomatic point of view is in Luciana Duranti, "Diplomatics: New Uses for an Old Science (Part III)," *Archivaria* 30 (Summer 1990): 4-20.

[25] For a discussion of the concept of fonds, see Terry Eastwood, ed., *The Archival Fonds: From Theory to Practice* (Ottawa: Bureau of Canadian Archivists, 1992).

[26] A special type of action is a *transaction*, which is an action between two or more persons, aiming to change the relationship existing between them. See also note 13 above.

[27] A juridical system is a social body organized according to a system of rules that it recognizes as binding. These rules are the *legal system* of the collectivity that abides by them. The legal system is made up of positive law, jurisprudence, customs, traditions, moral rules, and religious beliefs. The function of every record must be assessed in the context of the specific juridical system in which it is supposed to have effects. The legal system does not require the written form for every action. However, in literate societies, physical and juridical persons tend to act by means of records and with the support of records most of the time, because records facilitate the accomplishment of their daily affairs.

[28] In the sense used here, a document is information affixed to a medium in an objectified and organized way, according to specific written or unwritten rules of representation.

[29] Information is a meaningful group of data intended for communication, either across space or through time.

[30] Data is the smallest meaningful recorded facts.

[31] A procedure is a body of written or unwritten rules whereby an action is carried out, and comprises the formal steps to be undertaken to carry it out.

[32] The documentary context results from the totality of the archival bonds arising within an archival fonds.

[33] In this regard, another point to be made is that electronic records are not generated every time a database is queried, but only when this is done in the context of a business action and both the query and the reply become part of the records of such action. In other words, most electronic "transactions" are not related to specific business actions, as opposed to business activity in general, and do not generate records.

[34] Because of the archival bond, selection of records at the item level is considered unacceptable: it would destroy the archival bond and, consequently, the remaining records as records. Every selection, by hurting the integrity of the archival whole, would destroy parts of the documentary context, which is the only tangible expression of all the other contexts. However, selection carried out at the higher levels of aggregation does not interfere with the nature of the record or of the cause-effect connection between records; therefore, it is much more acceptable. Also because of the archival bond, archival description has been traditionally considered the primary way of perpetuating and authenticating the meaning of the records.

[35] This is particularly important, because the date of creation of the record is the most meaningful among the various dates that can be associated with a record (e.g. the date of compilation, of transmission, etc.). The date in which the archival bond arises is called the **archival date** and coincides with the time at which a record becomes effective, that is, begins to exercise its effects, or consequences.

[36] The reason obviously is that, if those sources are non-electronic, their content cannot change, its parts are permanently linked and their form will always remain the same. Thus, the reference made to a location in a document—a citation, that is—will always lead to the same text, or symbols, or images.

[37] Legibility of an electronic record is its ability to be accessed and read by a digital system different from the one that has produced it. Intelligibility of an electronic record is its ability to be understood in context. See Charles Dollar, "La memoria elettronica e la ridefinizione della preservazione," in *L'eclisse delle memorie*, T. Gregory and M. Morelli eds. (Roma, Bari: Editori Laterza, 1994), 174-178.

³⁸ The status of transmission of a record is its degree of perfection. There are three possible status of transmission: draft, original, and copy.

³⁹ A GIS has a medium (i.e., the actual hardware in which it is installed), a physical form (i.e., the architecture of the operating system), an intellectual form (i.e., the structure of the various layers that can be created within it), persons (i.e., the organization as the creator; the office competent for the activity using the system as author and originator; the individuals responsible for the office as writers; and the office itself as addressee); action (i.e., the activity supported by the system); context (i.e., the organization, the office, its competence, its procedure, the record of the same office that participate in the same activity); content (i.e., the data in the system), and archival bond (i.e., the relationship with other records in the same class expressed in a classificatory code).

⁴⁰ In fact, it does not matter whether the recordkeeping system is electronic or not, or whether a document is included in it by transmitting it electronically or by printing it out and inserting it in a dossier by hand. A document that is not set aside with the records of the creator has no archival bond and is not a record.

Chapter Two

¹ Terry Eastwood, "What is Archival Theory and Why is It Important?" *Archivaria* 37 (Spring 1994): 122-130.

² The science comprises the body of diplomatic theory, methods and practices, while the discipline consists of the rules that discipline the procedure of diplomatic criticism.

³ Luciana Duranti, "Diplomatics: New Uses for an Old Science," *Archivaria* 28 (Summer 1989): 17-18.

⁴ Abby Smith, "Introduction," in Council on Library and Information Resources, *Authenticity in a Digital Environment* (Washington, D.C.: CLIR, May 2000), vi.

⁵ Charles T. Cullen, "Authentication of Digital Objects: Lessons from a Historian's Research," in *Authenticity in a Digital Environment*, 1.

⁶ Ibid., 3.

⁷ Ibid., 5.

⁸ Peter B. Hirtle, "Archival Authenticity in the Digital Age," in *Authenticity in a Digital Environment*, 12-13.

⁹ David M. Levy, "Where is Waldo? Reflections on Copies and Authenticity in a Digital Environment," in *Authenticity in a Digital Environment*, 24.

¹⁰ Ibid., 26.

¹¹ A brief discussion of these concepts can be found in Luciana Duranti, "Reliability and Authenticity: The Concepts and Their Implications," *Archivaria* 39 (Spring 1995): 5-10.

¹² Luciana Duranti, "Diplomatics: New Uses for an Old Science (Part II)," *Archivaria* 29 (Winter 1989-90): 11. This quotation summarizes the points made by Stanley Raffel in *Matters of Fact* (London, Boston, and Henley: Routledge and Kegan Paul, 1979): 49-116.

¹³ The date in question is that of the compilation of the record. The dates of transmission and receipt and the archival date are functional to trace the routing of the record and verify its authenticity, but a record is to be considered complete in its intellectual form without them.

¹⁴ If the author of a record is an organization, an organ, a collegial or collective body, the writer will be the person articulating the content of the record in the name of the author. If the author is a "position," the writer will be the natural person covering such position. If the author is a natural person, the writer will coincide with the author.

¹⁵ As explained in the previous chapter, a medium, a physical and an intellectual form, five persons, an action, context, an archival bond and a content are the required components of any record.

¹⁶ This is just one indication of how important it is to keep distinct the author from the creator of the record.

¹⁷ One could imagine the draft of a policy sent to a higher body for approval, and say that this draft has crossed communication boundaries. In reality, it has not, because the lower body is acting as an arm of the higher body and the record has never left the author. In contrast, if the draft has been distributed to all the stakeholders for comments, what each one of them receives is an original draft, where the term draft refers to the degree of completion of the policy (i.e., the policy is incomplete and will never be transmitted to its addressees as guidance in its draft form), while the term original refers to the degree of completion of the record received by the stakeholder, which is complete for the purpose of generating comments.

¹⁸ It is an obvious, but little pondered, point that a document that cannot be proved authentic is not authentic, although might very well be genuine. Again, authenticity can only be ascertained through

the formal elements of the record, both physical and intellectual, including the annotations, which
represent the link between form and context.
[19] Clifford Lynch, "Authenticity and Integrity in the Digital Environment: An Exploratory Analysis of the
Central Role of Trust," in *Authenticity in a Digital Environment*, 33.
[20] Ibid., 34.
[21] Ibid., 40-41.

Chapter Three

[1] See above, p. 16.
[2] An agency should use, as a basis for thesaurus construction, the appropriate national or
international standard, e.g., ANSI/NISO Z39.19-1993 (Guidelines for the Construction, Format and
Management of Monolingual Thesauri), ISO 2788-1986 (Guidelines for the Establishment and
Development of Monolingual Thesauri), ISO 5964-1985 (Guidelines for the Establishment and
Development of Multilingual Thesauri); ISO-5963-1985 (Methods for Examining Documents,
Determining their Subjects and Selecting Indexing Terms.
[3] The thesaurus (known as the *STAR Thesdex*) was developed by the Nova Scotia government in
conjunction with the Standard for Administrative Records (STAR) scheme for the classification of the
records of the government of Nova Scotia and its agencies. The *Thesdex* (i.e., thesaurus and index)
is a collection of access points and a guide to terms used in STAR consisting of an alphabetical list of
terms used in the main groups, primaries, secondaries, and explanatory notes of the STAR
classification scheme, along with linkages to related terms. STAR is described in more detail in
Chapter 4.

Chapter Four

[1] See above, pp. 2-3.
[2]The connection between the integrity of the record and the integrity of the system is made explicitly
by the Uniform Law Conference of Canada (ULCC) in its Uniform Electronic Evidence Act. See
Uniform Law Conference of Canada, "Uniform Electronic Evidence Act Consultation Paper," March
1997, para. 3, <http://www.law.ualberta.ca/alri/ulc/> (March 1997), para. 24-26, 27. The Uniform
Electronic Evidence Act was adopted by the ULCC in 1998. A slightly revised version of this Act has
been incorporated into the Personal Information Protection and Electronic Documents Act, R.S.C.
2000, C. 5, p. 3.
[3] Access privileges should not be confused with access rules, which are understood to be the rules
governing access to records established in freedom of information and privacy laws and are not
specifically accounted for in the model since they constitute part of the control exercised by the
juridical system on the management of the archival fonds
[4] Modification of a record means a change to its content, content articulation or content configuration.
In the case of electronic forms, the filling in of the form constitutes the making of a record not a
modification of it. Once all the required fields have been filled in, the form may be treated as an entity
that should not be modified. It remains understood that, once a field has been filled in, it should not be
modifiable.
[5] The handling office/officer is the office or officer that is formally competent for carrying out the action
to which the record relates or for the matter to which the record pertains.
[6] An annotation added in the course of handling or managing the record is not considered a
modification.
[7] See above, pp. 29-30.
[8] See above, pp. 30-31.
[9] The descriptive elements of a classification scheme identified in this section are based on standards
for classifying and operational records developed in specific Canadian jurisdictions. These standards
include the Administrative Records Classification System (ARCS) and the Operational Records
Classification System (ORCS) developed for agencies of the government of British Columbia; as well
as the Standard for Administrative Records (STAR) and the Standard for Operational Records
(STOR) developed for agencies of the government of Nova Scotia. Although developed for public
agencies, the standards are equally applicable to private organizations. Both ARCS and STARS are
available online. See British Columbia, *Administrative Records Classification System (ARCS)*, located

at <http://www.bcarchives.gov.bc.ca/arcs/index.htm>; and Nova Scotia, *Standard for Administrative Records*, located at <http://www.nsarm.ednet.ns.ca/rm/star5/index.htm>.

[10] STAR refers to the largest grouping of records MAIN GROUPS, while ARCS and ORCS refer to it as SECTIONS.

[11] Penal Cassation, sect. V, 6 October 1987, cited in Maria Guercio, "Principi, metodi e strumenti per la formazione, conservazione e utilizzo dei documenti archivistici in ambiente digitale," *Archivi per la storia* XII, 1-2 (1999): 49.

[12] See above, pp. 31-32.

[13] A simple copy is a mere transcription of the content of the original. An imitative copy reproduces, either completely or partially, the content and form of the original record. A copy in the form of an original is identical to the original although generated subsequently. An authentic copy is a copy certified by authorized officials so as to render it legally admissible as evidence.

Conclusion

[1] United States, Department of Defense, Assistant Secretary of Defense for Command, Control, Communications, and Intelligence Design Criteria, *Standard for Electronic Records Management Software Applications* (DOD 5015.2-STD), June 2001.

[2] International Standards Organization, Technical Committee ISO/TC 46 Information and Documentation, Subcommittee 11, Archives/Records Management, *International Standards Organization International Standard (ISO/DIS 15489) Information and Documentation – Records Management* (Geneva: International Standards Organization, 2000).

[3] *Requirements for the Management of Electronic Records* (MoReq Specification), prepared by Cornwall Affiliates plc. (CECA-CEE-CEEA: Bruxelles-Luxembourg, 2001).

[4] MoReq Specification, "1.2 Purpose and Scope of this Specification."

Appendix A
Templates

TEMPLATE 1: WHAT IS A RECORD IN THE TRADITIONAL ENVIRONMENT?

I.   DIPLOMATICS

Record = archival document

Archival document = a document produced in the course of practical activity

Document = written evidence of juridical facts

Evidence = testimony of facts = conveyed observation of events

Written evidence = evidence produced on a medium by means of a writing instrument or of an apparatus for fixing data, images, or voices

Facts = human conduct or natural events

Juridical facts = facts whose occurrence is taken into consideration by the juridical system. Facts include acts.

Juridical system = a social group organized on the basis of a system of rules

System of rules = all the rules that are perceived as binding at any time and place by a given social group

Produced = made or received

Activity = a collection or sequence of acts aimed to one purpose

Practical activity = an activity whose purpose is not the activity itself but the production of effects capable of influencing situations

Therefore, a record is testimony, produced on a medium in the course of practical activity, of facts taken into consideration by the rules recognized as binding by a social group.

On the basis of this definition the **necessary components** of a record are:

1.   **medium** = the material support of the record's content, that is, of the testimony of facts

2.   **content** = the facts the record speaks of

3.   **form** = the way in which content is manifested = all the characteristics of a record determined by the application of the rules of representation of content typical of a given environment.

Form breaks down into:

a. **physical form** = the characteristics of the external appearance of the record, such as format, colours, etc. These characteristics are also called "extrinsic elements."
b. **intellectual form** = the characteristics of the internal composition of the record.
Intellectual form can be distinguished into:

i. **content configuration** = the mode of expression of the content: text, graphics, images, or a combination
ii. **content articulation** = the elements of the writing and their arrangement, that is, what determines the distinction between a letter and a memo or a chart and a map.
iii. **annotations** = additions to the content of the record made after its compilation

4.   **persons** = entities which the juridical system recognizes as having the capacity to act, that is, to generate consequences on the basis of the will. Persons can be either physical or juridical. Juridical persons are collections or successions of physical persons (also called moral persons or artificial persons). The existence of every record needs the concurrence of three persons:

a. **author** = the person competent for the creation of the record, which is issued by it or its command or in its name. The author of a record may coincide with the author of the action of which the record is the outcome, or may not.[1]
b. **addressee** = the person to whom the record is directed. The addressee of a record may coincide with the addressee of the action, or may not. The addressee is not necessarily the person to whom a record is delivered or transmitted.
c. **writer** = the person responsible for the intellectual form of the record. A modern term that expresses the same concept is **originator**. The writer cannot be a secretary or a clerk or a scribe.

There are other persons who can be involved in the creation of a record, but are not necessary to its existence. They are:

d. **countersigner** = the person who validates the form of the record, its procedure of creation, or its content. For example, the city-clerk signing a by-law.

e. **witness** = the person signing the record for the purpose of either conferring solemnity to it; authenticating the signature of the author, the content of the record, or its compilation; or stating that an act for which both oral and written form are required, such as an oath, took place in its presence.

5.   **acts** = acts are movements of the *will* aimed to create, maintain, modify or extinguish situations. A special type of act is a **transaction** = an act capable of changing the relationships between two or more persons

Therefore, the necessary components of a record are medium, content, form, persons, and acts. Intent of the author to transmit and capability to be transmitted are implied by the necessary existence of an addressee. Because of the necessary intent to transmit (over time or through space) **and capability of the record to be transmitted, readability to and intelligibility by the addressee at the moment of the creation of the record** (see the definition of the term "created" in the "archival science" section below) **are also implied.**

The minimum necessary requirements for a record to exist are:

a. **medium**
b. **content**
c. **form**
d. **persons**
e. **acts**

Implied requirements are:

f. **intent to be transmitted**
g. **capability to be transmitted**
h. **readability at the creation stage by the intended addressee**
i. **intelligibility at the creation stage by the intended addressee**

Question

Are actual **transmission** and **communication** necessary components? Proposition: not for a record to be "made," that is, to exist with the author; yes for a record to be "received," that is, to come into existence with the addressee. See below the definition of the term "creation."

II.   ARCHIVAL SCIENCE

Archival science does not define "a record", but "records," because it only deals with aggregations.

Records = archival documents

Archival documents = documents created by a physical or juridical person for the achievement of its purposes or in the exercise of its functions

Document = recorded information

Information = intelligence given = understanding conveyed

Recorded = affixed to a medium in a stable form

Created = made or received. A record is **made** when its compilation in its intended form is concluded and the record is set aside for transmission (over time or over space), reference and use, or subsequent action. A record is **received** when it reaches the intended addressee and is set aside for transmission, reference and use, or subsequent action. Initial preservation is necessary to the arising of documentary relationships.

Function = the whole of the activities aimed to one purpose. When such activities, or part of them, are assigned to a person, they constitute a **competence**

Therefore, records are documents made or received by a physical or juridical person as means and residue of its activity.

On the basis of this definition, we can add two other **necessary components** to those identified by diplomatics:

1.   **creator** = the physical or juridical person who makes or receives the records in the course of its activity

2.   **archival bond** = the relationships that, because of the circumstances of their creation, records have with their creator, with the activity in which they participate, and among themselves. The archival bond is *originary* (it comes into existence when the record is made or received), *necessary* (it exists for every record), and *determined* (it is characterized by the purpose of the record).

Therefore, archival documents or records are necessarily **composed of documents and the complex of their relationships.** Because of this, any document, of any nature, which acquires relationships with a group of archival documents or records, is to be considered a record itself, following the fundamental rule which governs every collectivity, according to which **each individual entity acquires the nature and characteristics of the whole to which it belongs.**

Is **order** a necessary component? The existence of an intellectual order is implied by the archival bond, thus order is a necessary consequence of the existence of the bond.

TEMPLATE 2: WHAT IS A COMPLETE RECORD IN THE TRADITIONAL ENVIRONMENT?

COMPLETE RECORD = a record that has all the elements of form required by the juridical system in which it is created. Completeness is conferred to a record by the presence of all required elements of its intellectual form, specifically the features of content articulation and the annotations.

Intellectual form = the characteristics of the internal composition of the record

They are, in any order:
1. **entitling** = name, title, capacity, or address of the physical or juridical person issuing the record or of which the author of the record is an agent (e.g. letterhead)
2. **title** = name of the record. It refers either to the form of the record (e.g. indenture, minutes) or to the act carried out by the record (e.g. agreement, oath of office)
3. **date** = place (topical date) and time (chronological date) of the compilation and/or issuing of the document and/or of the act which the record concerns
4. **superscription** = name of the author of the record and/or of the act (e.g. "I, John Smith, declare..." or "John Smith, of the first party"). In letters, it often takes the form of entitling.
5. **inscription** = name, title, and address of the addressee of the record and/or of the act
6. **salutation** = a greeting (e.g. "Dear sir")
7. **subject** = statement signifying what the record is about
8. **preamble** = statement expressing the ideal motivation of the act, or the ethical or juridical principles inspiring it, or the articles of law on which the action is based
9. **exposition** = statement of the concrete and immediate circumstances generating the record and/or the act
10. **disposition** = expression of the will or judgement of the author
11. **appreciation** = a wish for the realization of the disposition
12. **complimentary clause** = a brief formula expressing respect (e.g. "yours truly")
13. **attestation** = the subscription of those who took part in issuing the record (i.e. author, writer, countersigner, and/or witnesses). It might or might not take the form of signatures
14. **qualification of subscription(s)** = title and capacity of the subscriber(s)
15. **secretarial notes** = initials of typists, mention of enclosures, indication that the record is copied to other persons

Some other elements of content articulation are particular to certain record forms and contribute to their identification by being necessary to their completeness. They are:

16. **invocation** = mention of the higher power in the name of whom the type of act is carried out (e.g. "In the name of the law")
17. **formula perpetuitatis** = sentence declaring that the rights put into existence by the record are not circumscribed by time
18. **notification** = publication of the purport of the record (e.g. "Know you" as in a letters patent)
19. **corroboration** = enunciation of the means used to validate the record and guarantee its authenticity
20. **clause of injunction** = expression of the obligation of all those concerned to conform to the will of the author
21. **clause of prohibition** = prohibition to violate the enactment or oppose it
22. **clause of derogation** = expression of the obligation to respect the enactment notwithstanding other orders or decisions contrary to it, opposition, appeals, or previous dispositions
23. **clause of exception** = expression of the situations, conditions, or persons which are excepted from the enactment
24. **clause of obligation** = expression of the obligation of the parties to respect the act for themselves and for their successors or descendants
25. **clause of renunciation** = expression of the consent to give up a right or a claim
26. **clause of warning** = treat of punishment, should the enactment be violated
27. **promissory clause** = expression of the promise of a prize if the enactment is respected

The minimum required elements of content articulation for a record to be complete are:

       a. **date** (for identifying the topical and temporal context)
       b. **superscription** or **attestation** (for identification of the author)
       c. **inscription** (for identification of the addressee)
       d. **disposition** (for identification of the action)

With non textual records, that is, with graphic or image records, the minimum required elements of content articulation are:

       a. **date**
       b. **superscription** or **attestation**
       c. **inscription**
       d. **title** or **subject** (for identification of the content)

The **disposition** is represented by the graphics or the image.

In addition to these, other elements of content articulation are required within each given juridical system for each given record form.

Annotations = additions to the content of the record made after its compilation. They can be distinguished in categories in relation the procedural moment in the treatment of the affair in which they were added to the record in question:

Annotations added in the execution phase:

authentication = the express, legal recognition that a record or the signature(s) on it is what it purports to be (particular to certain record forms)
registration = the reference to a transcription of the record made in a register by an office different from the one creating the record (particular to certain record forms)

Annotations added during the **handling** of the record:

instructions = the mention of previous or following actions, directions for transmission, disposition, classification, etc.
dates of hearings or readings
signs besides the text = notations added by the reader, such as check marks, question marks, etc.

Annotations added during the **management** of the record:

registry number = the consecutive number assigned to incoming and outgoing mail in offices using the registry system
classification code = the code which identifies a record by its documentary relationships in the receiving and/or generating offices
cross-references = the indication of the classification code of related files
date of receipt = chronological date of the receipt of the record
name of recipient = name of the receiving office (usually affixed by a stamp) or individual.

The annotations required for a record to be complete are entirely dependent on the context of the creator

TEMPLATE 3: WHAT IS A RELIABLE RECORD IN THE TRADITIONAL ENVIRONMENT?

RELIABLE RECORD = a record endowed with trustworthiness. Specifically, trustworthiness is conferred to a record by its degree of **completeness** and the degree of control on its **creation procedure** and/or its **author's reliability**. Reliability of a record is not affected by its **mode, form,** or **state of transmission**.

Completeness = see the template entitled "What is a Complete Record in a Traditional Environment?"

Creation procedure = the procedure governing the formation of the record and/or its participation in the act.

Author's reliability = the competence of the author to issue the specific document and/or the degree to which an author can be trusted. The trustworthiness of an author can be ensured by:

    1. restricting the capacity to generate certain documents to certain persons
    2. requiring signatures
    3. giving responsibility to an author for reporting only a portion of a fact
    4. increasing the numbers of authors who report the same fact
    5. making the same record serve different purposes and users

Mode of transmission = the method by which a record is communicated (e.g. by hand, by regular mail, by FAX, by consigning it to the files and preserving it)

Form of transmission = the form that the record has when it is made or received

State of transmission = the primitiveness (i.e., order in time), completeness, and effectiveness (i.e., ability to achieve the purpose for which it was created) of a record when it is initially set aside after being made or received. There are three states of transmission: **draft, original,** and **copy.**

Draft = temporary version of a record, prepared for purposes of correction

Original = the first complete and effective record. It is possible to have **multiple originals** = records contemporarily created complete and effective, as in the case of reciprocal obligations, multiple addressees, or security needs.

Copy = a reproduction of a record in any state of transmission. There are different types of copies:

    simple copy = a transcription of the content of a record
    imitative copy = a reproduction of the form and content of a record

pseudo-original = an imitative copy made for purpose of deception
copy in the form of original = a complete and effective record, not the first to be created
authentic copy = a copy certified by an officer authorized to execute such function
inserts or **insets** = records entirely or partially quoted or reported in subsequent records in order to renew their effects or because they constitute precedent or serve as reference

While it can be assumed that an authentic copy is more reliable than a simple copy, this derives from the controlled creation procedure, not from the state of transmission. In fact, an authentic copy is as reliable as the record it reproduces.

Procedure = the body of written or unwritten rules which establishes the formal sequence of steps, stages or phases to be undertaken in carrying out an activity. A procedure needs to be distinguished from a **process** = a series of motions, or activities in general, carried out to set oneself to work and go on towards each formal step of a procedure (processes can create records, which would not be reliable, because what characterizes a process is its spontaneity and the absence of rules).

A record is as reliable as the procedure in which it takes part.

Reliable procedure = a procedure that has required phases, each with its own purpose, and that is controlled in each of its phases. A typical procedure has six possible phases:

initiative = the acts which start the mechanism of the procedure
inquiry = the acts which aim to the collection of information for decision
consultation = the collection of opinions and advice
deliberation = the act of deciding
deliberation control = control on the form and substance of the decision exercised by persons not involved in it
execution = the acts giving formal character to the transaction (validation, communication, notification, publication).

Of these six phases, the necessary ones for each procedure are:

a. **initiative**
b. **deliberation**
c. **execution** (in this phase, the one necessary element for reliability purposes is the **validation** = the conferring on the record of those extrinsic or intrinsic elements which make it effective, such as a signature, a seal, a stamp, or a signet)

For each procedure the number and type of formal phases vary. However many they are and whatever they are, in order to have a reliable procedure, they must be clearly identifiable according to the scheme presented above, expressly regulated, and controlled.

The records created in the course of a procedure have determined relationships with the acts of which they are part. These relationships can be of four types creating four different kinds of records:

> **dispositive** = records that substantiate the act
> **probative** = records that provide a posteriori evidence of completed acts
> **supporting** = records that provide written support for an oral activity
> **narrative** = records generated in the course of non-juridical activities

Dispositive and probative records are those whose **written form is required** by the juridical system. Supporting and narrative records are those whose written form is optional. Thus, dispositive and probative records need to be complete according to expressed rules in order to be reliable, while the reliability of supporting and narrative records can only be assessed on the grounds of their completeness (see the minimum requirements for completeness in the template entitled "What is a Complete Record in a Traditional Environment?"), their authors' reliability, and their **context of use** (i.e., the circumstances in which a record is actually used, including the reasons for such use), as showed by its relationships with the other records in the aggregations in which it belongs.

Each procedural phase is characterized by a predominance of one type or another of the types of records mentioned above. For example, the execution phase features a predominance of dispositive records.

CONCLUSION

The context of use of a record is expressed by its **annotations**, which represent the conjunction between elements of intellectual form and of procedure, as annotations are components of intellectual form added in the course of the creation procedure. Thus, they are a bridge between the completeness aspect of a record and the procedural control on its creation. This implies that a reliable record, whether dispositive, probative, supporting or narrative, must include in its intellectual form at least the following annotations:

> a. **name of recipient** = office or individual receiving the record
> b. **date of receipt** = (see template 2)
> c. **classification code** = (see template 2)

Other annotations are usually required by the specific juridical system and/or organizational context.

TEMPLATE 4: WHAT IS AN AUTHENTIC RECORD IN THE TRADITIONAL ENVIRONMENT?

AUTHENTIC RECORD = a record whose genuineness can be established. Authenticity is conferred to a record by its **mode, form,** and/or **state of transmission,** and/or **manner of preservation** and **custody.** In other words, an authentic record is one whose genuineness can be assumed on the basis of one or more of the following: mode, form and state of transmission, and manner of preservation and custody. (While a reliable record is one whose content you can trust, an authentic record is one whose provenance you can believe.)

Genuineness = the quality of a record that is truly what it purports to be

Mode of transmission: the method by which a record is communicated over space or time.

> **Requirements: security** = control on procedures of collection, delivery, reception, distribution and deposit of the record, on those carrying them out, and on the instruments or means used for carrying them out:
>
> > identification of hand carriers, and ground and air carriers
> > identification of mail office and mail clerks
> > identification of stamping and transmitting machines
> > routines for collecting records from the offices producing them
> > routines for classifying and/or registering outgoing records
> > routines for stamping and for consigning the records to the carrier
> > routines for date-stamping, classifying and/or registering incoming records
> > routines for distributing incoming records
> > routines for filing copies of outgoing records, incoming records, and internally produced records (after dating, classification and/or registration)

Form of transmission: the form that the record has when it is made or received.

> **Requirements:** presence of one or more of the following extrinsic or intrinsic elements:
>
> > watermarks
> > seals
> > signets
> > special signs
> > stamps
> > registration clause
> > authentication clause
> > registry number

classification number
entitling (e.g., letterhead) or superscription
date (topical and chronological)
addressee
corroboration
attestation(s)

Traditionally, the type of medium, its format, and its chemical composition, as well as the type, colour, and composition of the ink, have been used as means of authenticating records. While these characteristics of form are provided to the records in the course of their formation, rather than transmission or preservation, their explicit purpose is that of facilitating future authentication. It might also be noted that some elements of form, like attestation(s), serve reliability as well as authenticity.

State of transmission: the primitiveness, completeness, and effectiveness of a record when it is initially set aside after being made or received.

Requisites: genuineness is assumed a priori for

originals
copies in the form of original
authentic copies
inserts contained in originals, copies in the form of originals and authentic copies

Manner of preservation and **custody** = the way in which a record is maintained by its creator and/or legitimate successor.

Requisites: security = control on procedures of identification, filing, retrieval and access, storing, disposition, transfer, preservation, and conservation of the record, on those carrying them out, and on the instruments and means for carrying them out:

existence of a properly authorized records management office and records management officers
existence of a records keeping system including
    a records management written policy
    a records management written procedure
    an integrated classification/disposition system
    a registry system (optional)
    a controlled retrieval and access system
    an audit system
    secure records technologies
    records storage equipment and supplies
    a secure and natural place of preservation
    controlled environmental conditions

existence of proper procedures of transfer to the legitimate successor

existence of proper procedures of preservation and custody

    a secure and environmentally controlled building

    existence of guarantees of unbroken custody over time

    formally authorized and professionally qualified custodians

    a system of finding aids

    a controlled and secure system of consultation of the records

    a tracking system, a locator system

A non-authentic record can still be proved genuine by expert testimony or by witnesses present to its creation, but cannot be assumed such on its own account.

TEMPLATE 5: WHEN IS A RECORD CREATED IN THE ELECTRONIC ENVIRONMENT?

The necessary and sufficient requirements for any record to be created (made or received) are:

> a. **medium**
> b. **content** (facts or information)
> c. **form**
> d. **persons** (author, writer, addressee and creator)
> e. **acts**
> f. **archival bond**

The implied necessary and sufficient requirements for any record to be made are:

> g. **intent to be transmitted**
> h. **capability of being transmitted**
> i. **readability at the creation stage by the intended addressee**
> j. **intelligibility at the creation stage by the intended addressee**

The implied necessary and sufficient requirements for any record to be received are:

> k. **successful transmission**
> l. **readability at receipt**
> m. **intelligibility at receipt**

PROPOSITION: for any electronic record to be created all these requirements must be met.

a. **medium**
> The entity needs to be saved on a medium (on the hard drive, to a floppy disk, etc.) at least once when compiled or received.

b. **content**
> The entity needs to carry facts or information. This means that so-called "virtual records," which consist of pointers needed to create documents, have a content constituted by the information on the basis of which such documents are created. If these virtual entities meet all the other necessary and sufficient requisites, they are records of the sources used to create records. The same reasoning can be applied to metadata.

c. **form**
> The entity needs to have a readable and intelligible form. As the form is taken by the content that is affixed to the medium, it follows that the physical and intellectual form is stable at the moment of creation. (Specific elements of form are needed to have a complete, reliable, or authentic record.)

d. persons

The entity needs to have an author, a writer or originator, an addressee, and a creator. **Do these persons need to be human beings?** No. **Do these persons need to be juridical persons?** Not all of them, only the author and/or the creator. They need to be recognised by the juridical system as capable of acting, that is, as having a will that can create, maintain, modify, or extinguish situations. For example, if an expert system makes decisions capable of generating consequences recognised as such by the juridical system, it has to be considered a juridical person. However, a database, such as a GIS, is not a juridical person, having no will.

e. acts

The entity needs to be directly connected with some action. Specifically, it must either carry out an action (e.g., a job advertisement sent via E-Mail), provide evidence of an action already carried out (e.g., report of a job interview), provide support to an action (e.g., questions for the interview prepared ahead of time), or provide information on which to base action (e.g., the applicant's curriculum vitae). Observational databases, for example, do not contain entities directly connected with action. However, entities extracted from such databases can come into direct connection with action. (This absolves us from an item by item examination of databases.)

f. archival bond

The entity needs to be part of the whole of the documents made or received in the course of the activities of its creator. This implies that the entity has established and unique relationships with those documents. These relationships arise when the entity is set aside for use (for example, filed in a directory, in an E-Mail file, registered, classified, etc.).

g. transmission

The entity needs to be created with the intent and the capacity of being communicated.

It is essential to underline that the requirements discussed above must coexist in any given entity for it to be considered a record. For example, if an individual queries a database and retrieves an "answer," both query and answer (which obviously have been transmitted) can be considered record(s) only if their content is saved by that individual to a medium, in a readable and intelligible form, and connected by an archival bond (that is, by saving them to the proper file, or assigning them a classification or registration code) to the specific activity that they were meant to support. In this example, the action is entirely carried out by the person who sends the query and retrieves the answer, who would therefore be the author, writer, addressee and creator of the record(s) in question. This act (retrieving information) cannot be considered a transaction because it is not aimed to change, maintain, extinguish or create relationships or situations among two or more persons, as only one person is involved.

TEMPLATE 6: WHEN IS A COMPLETE RECORD CREATED IN THE ELECTRONIC ENVIRONMENT?

The necessary and sufficient elements of intellectual form for a traditional textual record to be complete are:

> a. **date** (time and place)
> b. **superscription** or **attestation** (name or signature of author)
> c. **inscription** (name of addressee)
> d. **disposition** (action)

The necessary and sufficient elements of intellectual form for traditional non-textual records to be complete are:

> a. **date**
> b. **superscription** or **attestation**
> c. **inscription**
> d. **title** and/or **subject** (identification of content)
> e. **disposition** (the image, the graphic, the numerals, etc.)

PROPOSITION: for any electronic record to be complete, elements of intellectual form comparable to those required for traditional records are necessary, but they might not be sufficient.

TEXTUAL RECORDS IN ELECTRONIC FORM

a. **date**

> The record must have a date, because the mention of the time and place of the record's creation captures the relationship between its author/writer and the fact/act in question, and this relationship becomes something the record talks about. With traditional records, the date is usually included in the record when its compilation begins, and appears on the top or bottom of the record. With electronic records, the date is usually automatically added by the electronic system to electronic messages, when these pass through the buffer, that is, after their compilation is concluded and the transmission command has been given. The date appears on the first line of the header, and includes the time of receipt of the message in addition to that of delivery, but does not include the place. With other electronic applications, the time is added by the system if this has the ability to control the "version" of the documents moved through it, or is included by the author/originator when the document is finished.
> **Therefore, with electronic records, the chronological date must include the time of transmission** (to an internal and/or external addressee) **and time of receipt. Moreover, the topical date** (the

mention of the place where the document is made and/or from where it is transmitted) **is also necessary for a record to be complete.**

b. superscription or attestation

The record must include the name of the author, because this element assigns responsibility for its content. With traditional records, the name of the author may appear in the letterhead (entitling), in the initial wording of the text (superscription), and/or at the bottom of the document as a signature, a symbol, or a signet (attestation). The signature or its equivalent attests that the record is adequate, and this attestation becomes the most important fact about the record. With electronic records, the name of the person releasing the record (not necessarily its author) is usually automatically added by the electronic system to messages after their compilation is concluded and the transmission command has been given. Any electronic record system can only automatically include among the intellectual elements of form the electronic address from which a message is sent. This address might be that of the author/writer of the message, or of its originator (be this person aware or not of it). Juridically, the person from whose address the message is sent is its author and writer, unless an attestation is attached to the record that would unequivocally demonstrate who its author/writer is, such as an electronic seal. The subscription (that is, the mention of the name of the author/writer at the end of the record) is not to be considered an attestation, because anyone could type any name. While the name of the person from whose address the record is sent, by automatically appearing on the header, carries with itself some authority, and therefore can be compared with an entitling or letterhead, it can never have an attestation function.

Therefore, with electronic records, the attestation of the author and an entitling showing the name of the originator are necessary for completeness. (If security is such that nobody other than the electronic address holder, that is, the originator, can have access to that address for sending messages, then the entitling does acquire a superscription function, but never an attestation function).

c. inscription

The record must include the name of the addressee, because it needs to be manifested, that is, transmitted or intended for transmission to some person in order to come into existence. With traditional records, the name of the addressee is usually expressed in the initial part of the record, whereas the names of those to whom the record is copied **(receivers)** is expressed in a separate section, usually at the end. With electronic records, the name of the addressee(s) is usually included in the header of electronic messages as well as the names of the receivers. However, when a message is forwarded to a list of addressees and/or receivers that resides in the electronic system, such list may not appear in the header of the record.

Therefore, with electronic records, the name of all addressees and receivers must be included for completeness, making sure that the two groups are formally distinguished. (While the names of the addressees need to be in the body of the record, that is, constitute an intrinsic element of form, the names of the receivers can simply be linked to the record and constitute an extrinsic element of form, which would fall into the category "annotations").

d. disposition

The record must include the disposition, that is, the expression of the will or judgement of the author, because this is the reason why the record is created in the first place. With traditional records, the disposition is usually introduced by a verb able to communicate the nature of the action and the function of the record. With electronic records, there is no difference.

Therefore, with electronic records, a message expressive of the will or judgement of the author is necessary for completeness.

NON-TEXTUAL RECORDS IN ELECTRONIC FORM

a. date

As with textual records in electronic form, **chronological** and **topical dates are necessary for a non-textual record in electronic form to be complete.**

b. superscription or attestation

As with textual records in electronic form, **both an entitling and the attestation of the author are necessary for a non-textual record in electronic form to be complete.**

c. inscription

As with textual records in electronic form, **the name of all addressees must be included in each non-textual record in electronic form for it to be complete, while the names of the receivers need only to be linked to it.**

d. title and/or subject

The record must include a title, providing its name, and/or a subject, describing its content. The title or the subject should include the date of the event, fact, or act represented, if different from the date of the record. While traditional non-textual records do not always have a title or subject, **non-textual records in electronic form, just like the textual ones, always include a one line title** (which is usually called "file name") that is often the subject of the record. This is not sufficient for either textual or non-textual records.

Therefore, with both textual and non-textual electronic records, a title and/or subject that properly describe the record and its matter are necessary for completeness.

e. disposition

With non-textual records, the disposition is represented by the graphics or images contained in the record.

CONCLUSION

All complete electronic records, whether textual or non-textual, must include the following elements of intellectual form:

    1. Chronological date (of both transmission and receipt)
    2. Topical date
    3. Entitling (originating address)
    4. Attestation (name of author/writer)
    5. Addressee(s)
    6. Receivers (name of copied persons)
    7. Title or subject
    8. Disposition

TEMPLATE 7: HOW IS A RECORD CREATED RELIABLE IN THE
ELECTRONIC ENVIRONMENT?

**The reliability of any record depends on its degree of completeness, degree
of control on its creation procedure, and/or its author's reliability.**

An electronic record is to be considered **complete** when it includes the eight
elements of intellectual form.

However, for purposes of reliability, some of those elements, together with
others, need to be also included in attachment to the record, called the
document profile. For an electronic record, the document profile is the container
of all annotations, but also of some elements of intellectual form, as follows:

> every record made, in order to be considered complete and transmitted
> internally, must include in its document profile:
>
> > **date**
> > **time**
> > **author**
> > **addressee**
> > **subject**
>
> every record received from outside, in order to be either filed or further
> transmitted, must include in its document profile:
>
> > **date of receipt**
> > **time of receipt**
> > **date of further transmission**
> > **time of further transmission**
> > **author**
> > **addressee**
> > **classification code**
> > **registry number (if applicable)**

The elements related to the control of **creation procedure** that have been
identified for traditional records are:

> the express regulation of three procedural phases, that is, of initiative,
> deliberation, and execution, and
> the required addition to the record of at least three annotations, that is,
> name of recipient, date of receipt, and classification code.

With electronic records, the second of the above requirements is satisfied in the
document profile, while the first requirement must be preceded by a series of
other controls, as follows:

identification of the communication networks, electronic record system and software to be used

identification of the users of the electronic record system and of their individual privileges within the system on the basis of the administrative competence of each of them and of the organization of their work

definition within the system of the boundaries of **general space, group space**, and **individual space**

> **general space** = that part of the system that is accessible to all members of the organization, managed according to established record making and recordkeeping rules by the competent staff, and that contains the central filing system of the organization, including the linkages with related records in other media. The primary characteristic of the general space is that no record that has crossed its boundaries can thereafter be manipulated.

> **group space** = that part of the system that is accessible to all the individuals who share the same competence, horizontally or vertically, temporarily or permanently. This is the space containing many draft versions of the same record, comments, notations, etc.

> **individual space** = that part of the system that is accessible only to individual members of the organization. The individual space within the organization's records system must be distinguished from the personal, **private space** of the individual, which should have also a different electronic address. This private space may lie beyond the concerns of the organization

identification of a secure way of entering the system, such as cards with magnetic stripe, voice print, finger print, etc.

In addition, it is essential to distinguish within each creating context between those procedures that can be embedded in the electronic systems as automated workflows, and those that can only be regulated by a code of administrative procedure external to the electronic system. Reliability is served by either or both methods of procedural control.

As mentioned earlier, the document profile can be used as a primary instrument for making a record reliable. A complementary instrument to the document profile is constituted by the **metadata**, that is, data on the creation and use of the records within the system that are automatically generated and preserved by the system and transparent to the user.

The elements related to the‚**author's reliability** are procedural ones, which are expressed in traditional records by the signature of the author.

With electronic records, the procedural elements that guarantee the author's reliability are best expressed in the control of the access by the users - as said earlier. This control is exercised by limiting and identifying the persons who can have access to the system, and, once inside it, who can read what, who can interact with what and in which way, etc. This control is also exercised by enabling the electronic system to keep an audit trail of the uses made of the system.

As it has been seen, when procedures of creation control are in place, the control on user's access to specific applications is an integral part of them. The control on user's access has the purpose of making the persons competent for the actions in which the records take part responsible for generating them, and accountable for their contents. This is because reliability is linked to administrative competence for action, not to security, which is an authenticity issue.

TEMPLATE 8: HOW IS AN ELECTRONIC RECORD GUARANTEED AND/OR PROVED AUTHENTIC?

Authenticity is conferred to a record by its mode, form, and/or state of transmission, and/or manner of preservation and custody.

In electronic systems as well as in traditional records systems, authenticity is ensured by enforcing sophisticated administrative procedures, employing difficult to reproduce technical instruments, and installing security systems.

Mode of transmission

The method by which a record is communicated over space or time needs to be secure in order to guarantee the authenticity of the record. This security can be achieved as follows:

> articulation of the circumstances and manner of transmitting records from one space to another either automatically or manually, and of receiving records from outside in any of the spaces

> inclusion in the system of an audit trail capability that keeps a trace of every transmission (date, time, persons, subject)

Form of transmission

The form the record has when it is made or received can also guarantee the authenticity of records. Traditionally, authenticity relies on extrinsic or intrinsic characteristics such as watermarks, seals, etc. In the electronic environment, every record made, in order to be transmitted externally, must have a document profile attached to it that must include:

> **date**
> **time**
> **author**
> **addressee**
> **subject**
> **classification code**
> **registry number (if applicable)**
> **corroboration (indication of the protection used)**

> every record made, in order to be transmitted in a completely secure way, must be protected by:

>> **date stamping** or

cryptographed seal

a simple way of providing records with **special signs** difficult to imitate is by accompanying the subscription on the record with some drawing and/or motto that can only identify specific persons

State of transmission

Authenticity relates to state of transmission in the measure in which it can be assumed for originals, copies in the form of originals, authentic copies, and inserts contained in originals, copies in the form of originals, and authentic copies. Thus, with electronic records, every record received from outside is to be considered an original at the moment in which it is physically affixed to the system, being the first complete record to reach the effects for which it was transmitted. In order to protect the characteristics of this original record, it is essential to attach to it a complete document profile before the record is handled for the transaction of the affairs to which it relates, and to include it in the central files in the general space.

every record transmitted from the individual to the group space is to be considered an original as well.

most records moving within the work space are drafts. To allow for its identification, each draft must have attached a document profile indicating date, time, author, number of version, and any other relevant data, such as names of other persons consulted about it outside the work space. Other records are comments on drafts, and must be considered originals because each comment is a first, complete and effective record on its own. This means that each comment has to have a document profile too with date, time, author, and the reference to the draft, including its version number, to which it relate. Still other records are copies in the form of originals of the records on file used as reference, or forwarded to the group for taking action. Each final complete record transmitted to the general space must have the appropriate profile as defined above; it leaves the group space as the final draft and is received in the general space as an original. This original is then protected by adding classification code etc. to the profile. If it is meant to be sent outside, the protective measures mentioned above must be added; otherwise it may be filed.

A specific issue that needs to be addressed is that of **inserts**. Inserts are records entirely quoted (if textual) or reported (if images or graphics) in subsequent original records in order to renew their effects, or because they constitute precedents of the actions to which the subsequent originals refer. While the authenticity of the record containing the insert can be guaranteed by using any of the measures described in this document or a combination thereof, the authenticity of the insert itself cannot be ensured, as it depends on the reliability of the author of the record containing it and on the authenticity of the record from which the insert is made.

Manner of preservation and custody

In addition to all the requisites identified for records created in the traditional environment, it is necessary to establish specific ones for the secure preservation and custody of electronic records, such as:

> backward and forward compatibility for the technology chosen for preservation purposes
> a routine for making backup copies of the records in the system
> a routine according to which master copies of the record are preserved in a climatically suitable and physically secure environment, while other copies are reserved for use and made easily available to the users
> a routine for authenticating master copies
> a system of regular recopying and/or migration

Appendix B
Activity Models

INTRODUCTION

This introduction aims to explain the methodology of modeling used by the project.

It employed a standard modeling technique called IDEF or Integrated Definition Language. IDEF was familiar to the Records Management Task Force (RMTF) of the United States Department of Defense (DoD) with whom we worked to develop these activity models.

The first step requires definition of the purpose, scope, and viewpoint of the modeling. The **purpose** of the modeling is to define the activities engaged in during the genesis and preservation of an agency's archival fonds. In this context, archival fonds is the whole of the records created by an agency and preserved. Agency is defined as an administrative body having the delegated authority to act competently as an agent of a higher authority. For example, DoD is an agency of the Government of the United States. The **scope** is to control records according to the agency's mandate using the principles of archival science. The **viewpoint** is that of the records' creator, where the records' creator is an agency. Essentially, then, the team set out to model all of the activities involved in managing the whole of the records under the control and care of an agency. For the obvious reason of the RMTF's interest in establishing policies and procedures for management of all of the records, both electronic and non-electronic, of DoD, we chose to model from the viewpoint of an agency. However, the results of the work could easily be applied to the whole of an organization, where appropriate, given the scale of the organization. It should also be noted that the team did not set out to model the activities involved in management of records transferred to an entity responsible for permanent or long-term preservation of records.

The models or diagrams themselves represent the context of an activity, what goes into it (the inputs), is transformed during it, and comes out of it (the outputs). The context of the activity is characterized by identifying and describing the **controls** or constraints on it that need to be taken into account on the one hand, and the **mechanisms**, that is, the technological and human resources needed to perform the activity, on the other. The **inputs** are the things that initiate or trigger the activity and that are transformed by it. The **outputs** are the things brought about by the activity, its results. The aim of the modeling is to decompose or break down the master activity, in this case the activity of managing an archival fonds, into all of its relevant sub-activities, in order to make it clear what is to be done and to show the relationships among connected activities. The highest level activity is called the parent, while the lower level activities are called children, which, when further decomposed, become parents, and so on as long as decomposition is fruitful.

The controls are represented on the diagrams as downward pointing arrows, the mechanisms as upward pointing arrows, the inputs as arrows pointing from left to right, and the outputs as arrows pointing from right to left. All the arrows are labelled with a term of one or more words to describe the entity concerned. Where an arrow is bracketed, it means that the control or mechanism concerned applies to all lower levels, and therefore will not be shown at those lower levels. This feature of the models is called tunneling. All the terms used on the diagram are defined in a glossary, which is reproduced in Appendix C. Each level of decomposition is called a "node," is numbered according to its position in the hierarchy of activities, and is assigned a unique title reflecting the activity involved. Thus, one reads the diagrams, in conjunction with the glossary, as a series of interconnected representations of all the activities involved in managing the records of an agency.

For example, the highest level model, for **Manage Archival Fonds**, indicates that four conditions constrain the activity of managing the records of an agency. First, one must observe certain principles and follow certain methods commonly understood to constitute proper practice in the treatment of records, which we have indicated as "archival science" on the diagram. Archival science is defined as: "The concepts, principles, and methodologies governing the treatment of records. It includes the concepts, principles, and methodologies defined by diplomatics." For example, it is a cardinal principle of archival science that each record is related to others participating in the same action, transaction, matter, or affair. The definitions of each of the other terms of the diagram may be consulted in the glossary. The other controls are fairly straightforward. The constitutional, legal, and traditional makeup of the society where the records are kept will determine or influence certain elements of practice, as will the nature of the creator's mandate and functions and any applicable national or international standards. These controls are tunnelled because they will apply at all lower levels. In some cases, particular controls are identified at lower levels, especially those developed as part of the activity of setting records management policy. As well, the mechanisms, at this general level, are relatively broadly construed as human resources, tools, and facilities needed to carry out the management of records. At lower levels, more particular mechanisms may also be identified.

The inputs and outputs at this highest level are also appropriately characterized in general terms, which can be seen in more detail by reading the glossary. However, the full range of understanding of this highest level diagram can only be understood by reading the full range of diagrams produced by the decomposition of the parent into its various children, and those in some cases into their children. An overview of the entire decomposition is shown in the second diagram, called the "node tree." Among other things, this diagram shows that the four children of the parent activity "Manage Archival Fonds" are "Manage Archival Framework," "Create Records," "Handle Records," and "Preserve Records." In the work of characterizing these four sub-activities and their respective children, it was considered important to write rules to guide the conduct of the activities. The rules, which are referred to many times in chapters 4, 5 and 6, appear in Appendix D. The glossary and the rules in fact act as a compendium of references to help explain the diagrams and the complex thinking behind their generation.

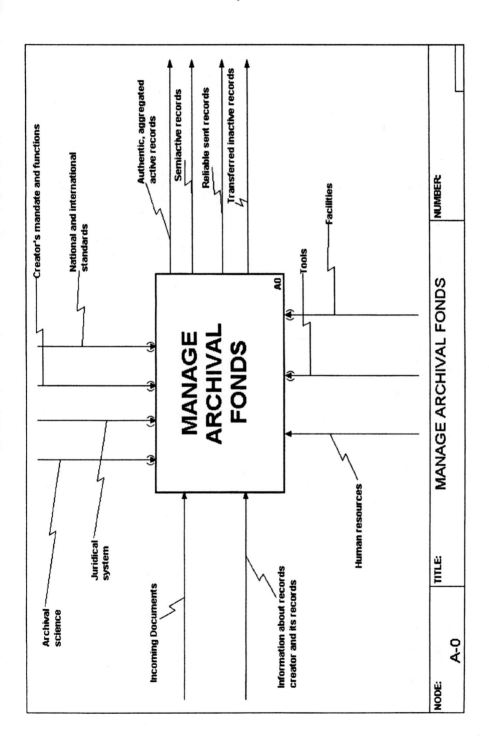

Creator's mandate and functions

National and international standards

Archival science

Juridical system

Incoming Documents

Information about records creator and its records

Human resources

MANAGE ARCHIVAL FONDS

A0

Authentic, aggregated active records

Semiactive records

Reliable sent records

Transferred inactive records

Tools

Facilities

NODE: A-0   TITLE: MANAGE ARCHIVAL FONDS   NUMBER:

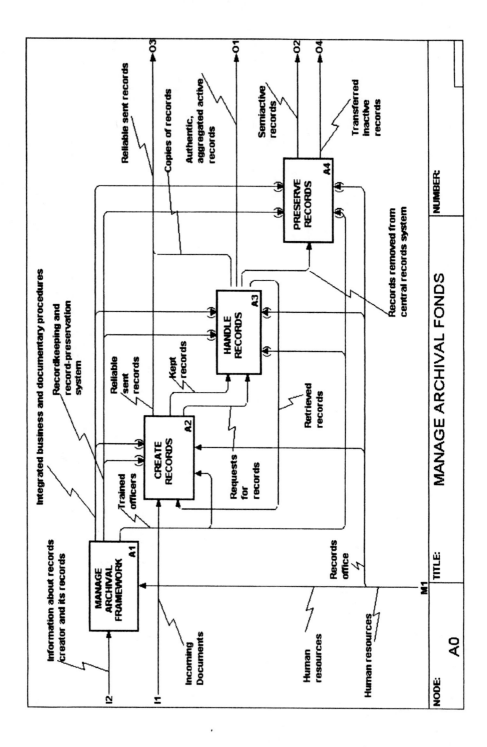

NODE: TITLE: MANAGE ARCHIVAL FONDS   NUMBER:

AO

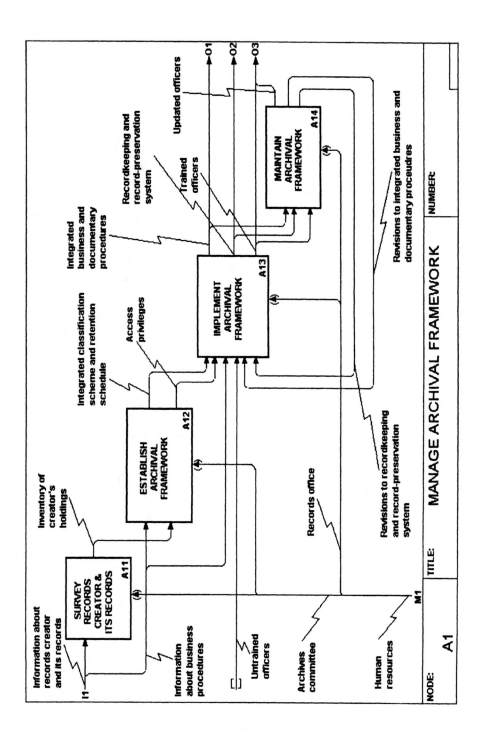

MANAGE ARCHIVAL FRAMEWORK

NODE: A1   TITLE: NUMBER:

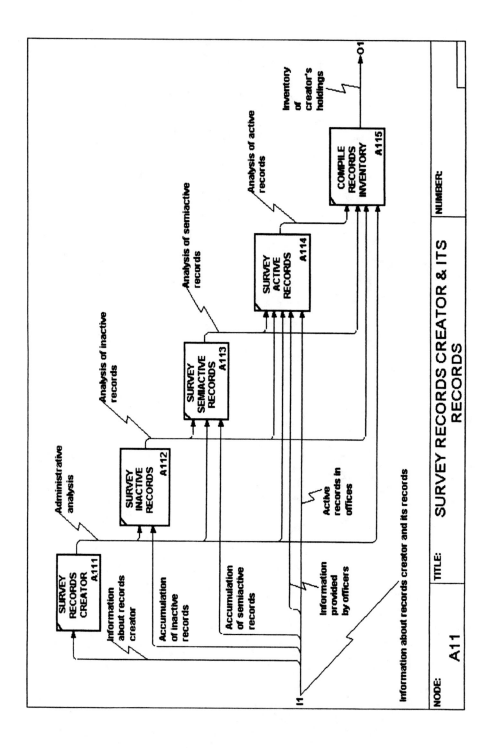

NODE: A11   TITLE: SURVEY RECORDS CREATOR & ITS RECORDS   NUMBER:

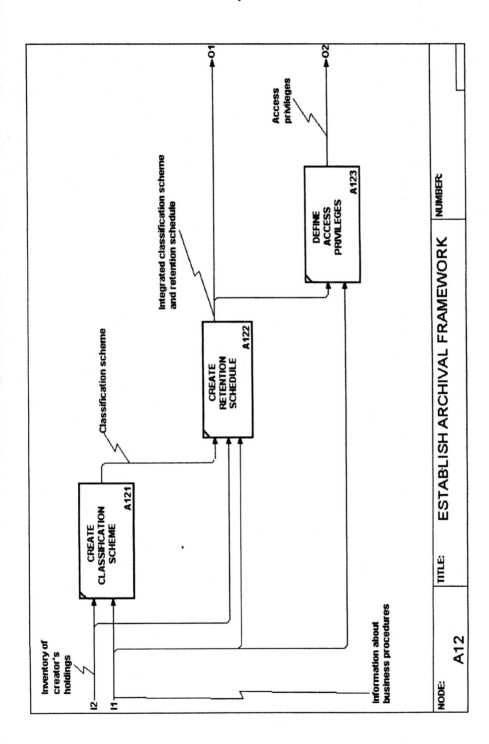

NODE: A12   TITLE: ESTABLISH ARCHIVAL FRAMEWORK   NUMBER:

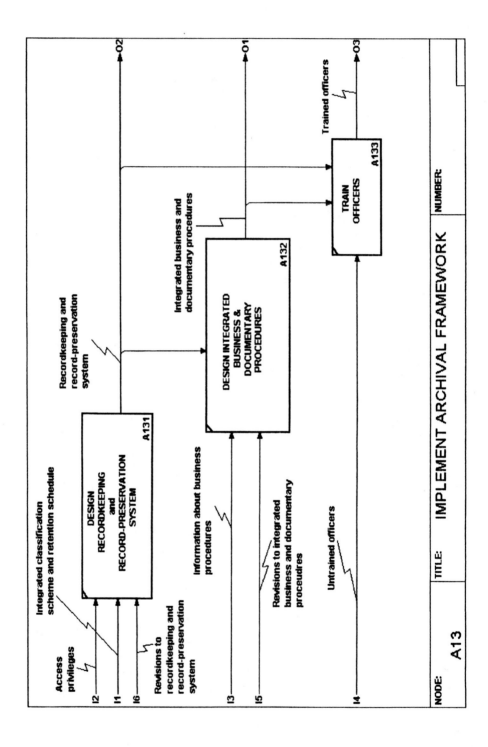

NODE: A13   TITLE: IMPLEMENT ARCHIVAL FRAMEWORK   NUMBER:

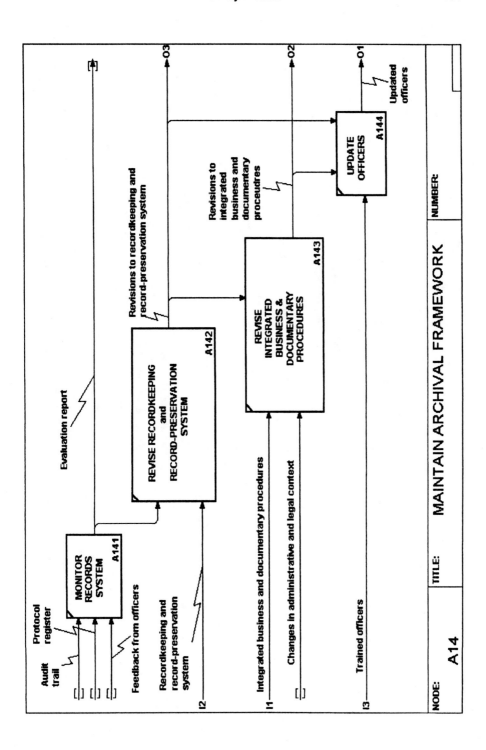

Audit trail

Protocol register

Feedback from officers

Recordkeeping and record-preservation system

Integrated business and documentary procedures

Changes in administrative and legal context

Trained officers

MONITOR RECORDS SYSTEM

A141

Evaluation report

REVISE RECORDKEEPING and RECORD-PRESERVATION SYSTEM

A142

Revisions to recordkeeping and record-preservation system

REVISE INTEGRATED BUSINESS & DOCUMENTARY PROCEDURES

A143

Revisions to integrated business and documentary proceudres

UPDATE OFFICERS

A144

Updated officers

NODE: A14

TITLE: MAINTAIN ARCHIVAL FRAMEWORK

NUMBER:

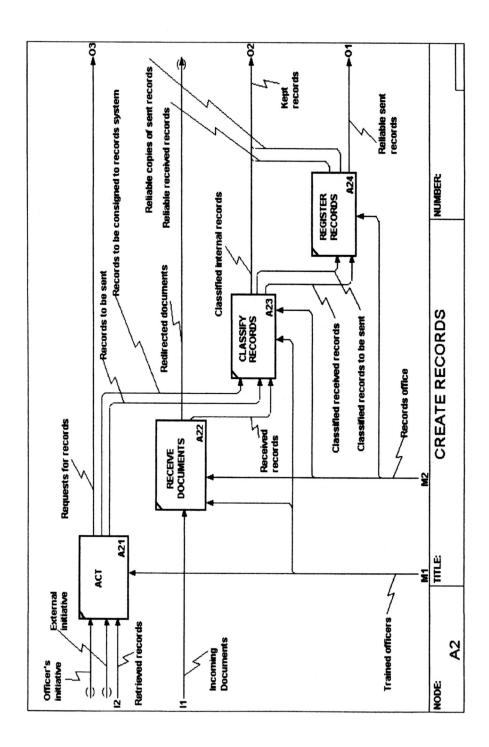

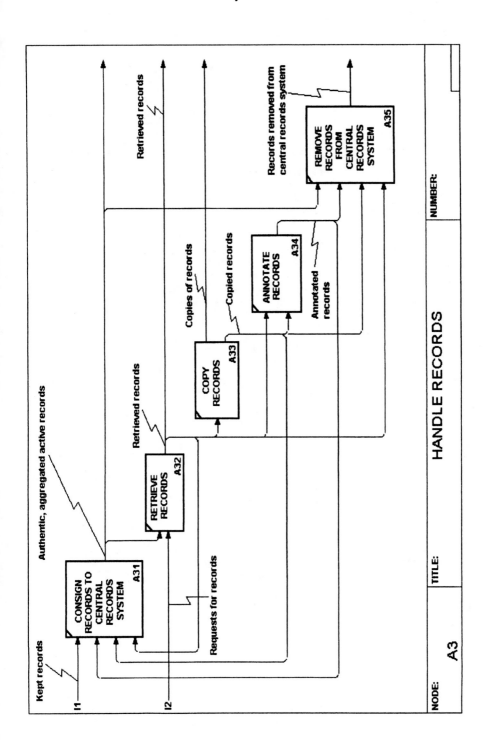

Kept records

Authentic, aggregated active records

Retrieved records

Retrieved records

Copies of records

Copied records

Annotated records

Records removed from central records system

Requests for records

I1

I2

CONSIGN RECORDS TO CENTRAL RECORDS SYSTEM
A31

RETRIEVE RECORDS
A32

COPY RECORDS
A33

ANNOTATE RECORDS
A34

REMOVE RECORDS FROM CENTRAL RECORDS SYSTEM
A35

NODE: A3   TITLE: HANDLE RECORDS   NUMBER:

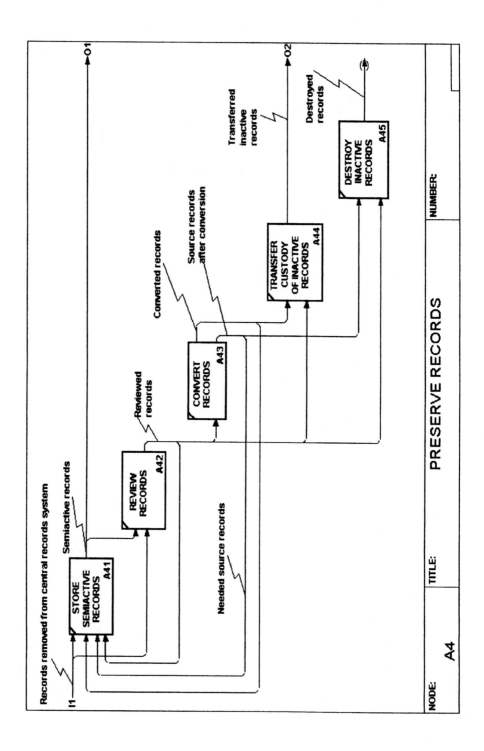

Records removed from central records system

Semiactive records

I1

STORE
SEMIACTIVE
RECORDS
A41

REVIEW
RECORDS
A42

Reviewed
records

CONVERT
RECORDS
A43

Converted records

Source records
after conversion

Needed source records

TRANSFER
CUSTODY
OF INACTIVE
RECORDS
A44

Transferred
inactive
records

DESTROY
INACTIVE
RECORDS
A45

Destroyed
records

O1

O2

NODE: A4   TITLE: PRESERVE RECORDS   NUMBER:

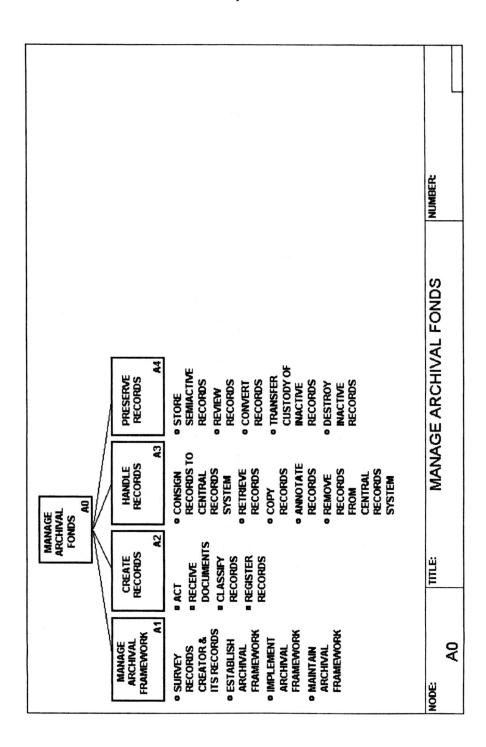

MANAGE ARCHIVAL FONDS
A0

MANAGE ARCHIVAL FONDS
A0

MANAGE ARCHIVAL FRAMEWORK
A1

CREATE RECORDS
A2

HANDLE RECORDS
A3

PRESERVE RECORDS
A4

A1 — MANAGE ARCHIVAL FRAMEWORK
- SURVEY RECORDS CREATOR & ITS RECORDS
- ESTABLISH ARCHIVAL FRAMEWORK
- IMPLEMENT ARCHIVAL FRAMEWORK
- MAINTAIN ARCHIVAL FRAMEWORK

A2 — CREATE RECORDS
- ACT
- RECEIVE DOCUMENTS
- CLASSIFY RECORDS
- REGISTER RECORDS

A3 — HANDLE RECORDS
- CONSIGN RECORDS TO CENTRAL RECORDS SYSTEM
- RETRIEVE RECORDS
- COPY RECORDS
- ANNOTATE RECORDS
- REMOVE RECORDS FROM CENTRAL RECORDS SYSTEM

A4 — PRESERVE RECORDS
- STORE SEMIACTIVE RECORDS
- REVIEW RECORDS
- CONVERT RECORDS
- TRANSFER CUSTODY OF INACTIVE RECORDS
- DESTROY INACTIVE RECORDS

NODE: TITLE: MANAGE ARCHIVAL FONDS   NUMBER:
A0

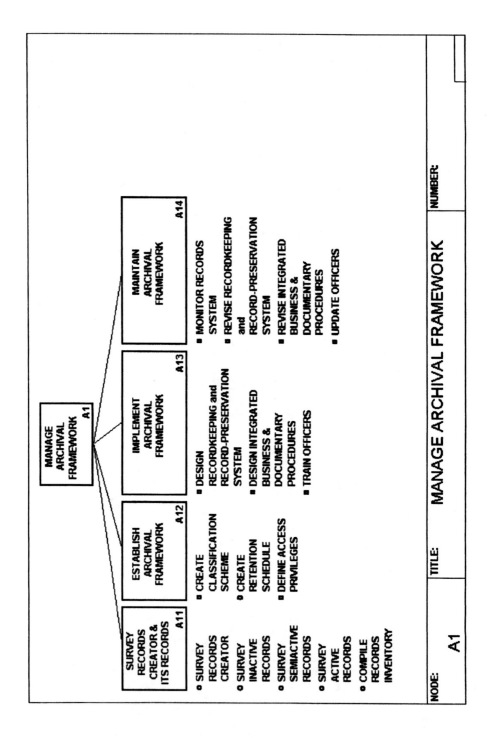

MANAGE ARCHIVAL FRAMEWORK

MANAGE ARCHIVAL FRAMEWORK — A1

SURVEY RECORDS CREATOR & ITS RECORDS — A11
- SURVEY RECORDS CREATOR
- SURVEY INACTIVE RECORDS
- SURVEY SEMIACTIVE RECORDS
- SURVEY ACTIVE RECORDS
- COMPILE RECORDS INVENTORY

ESTABLISH ARCHIVAL FRAMEWORK — A12
- CREATE CLASSIFICATION SCHEME
- CREATE RETENTION SCHEDULE
- DEFINE ACCESS PRIVILEGES

IMPLEMENT ARCHIVAL FRAMEWORK — A13
- DESIGN RECORDKEEPING and RECORD-PRESERVATION SYSTEM
- DESIGN INTEGRATED BUSINESS & DOCUMENTARY PROCEDURES
- TRAIN OFFICERS

MAINTAIN ARCHIVAL FRAMEWORK — A14
- MONITOR RECORDS SYSTEM
- REVISE RECORDKEEPING and RECORD-PRESERVATION SYSTEM
- REVISE INTEGRATED BUSINESS & DOCUMENTARY PROCEDURES
- UPDATE OFFICERS

NODE: A1   TITLE: MANAGE ARCHIVAL FRAMEWORK   NUMBER:

Appendix C
Glossary Of Terms Used In
Activity And Entity Models

FORMAT OF THIS GLOSSARY

The first line gives the defined term. Terms for activities, entities and instances of entities are shown in upper case letters. ICOMs (controls, mechanisms, inputs, outputs) and terms used in the activity model or in procedural rules are shown in mixed case.

The second line gives the location(s) on the models where the term is used.

Then the term is defined. Words that appear within definitions and are further defined are underlined and italicized, regardless of their singular or plural form.

Access privileges
ICOM: A1/A12/A13
The authority to compile, classify, annotate, read, retrieve, transfer, and destroy *records*, granted to *officers* within an *agency*.

Accumulation of inactive records
ICOM A11
The *inactive records* of the *agency*, whether maintained within the *agency* or by the *competent archival body*.

Accumulation of semi-active records
ICOM A11
The *semi-active records* of the *agency*.

ACT (v.)
Activity: A2 (A21)
To give origin to an *act (n.)*

ACT (n.)
Entity
The conscious exercise of will by an *officer* of the *records creator* or by an external person aimed to create, maintain, modify or extinguish situations. There are two types of act: a *mere act* and a *transaction*. Alias: *action*.

Action
Entity Model: definition of *ACT (n)*
The conscious exercise of will by an *officer* of the *records creator* or by an external person aimed to create, maintain, modify or extinguish situations. There are two types of act: a *mere act* and a *transaction*. Alias: *act*.

Active records
Activity model definition of *Authentic, aggregated active records*
Records which are needed by the *records' creator* for the purposes of carrying out the *actions* for which they were created.

Active records in offices
ICOM: A11
Active records which are kept by the handling *offices/officers*.

Administrative analysis
ICOM: A11
See rules in the text of the report related to the activity *SURVEY RECORDS CREATOR*.

AGENCY
Context entity in entity model
Activity Model: (Title, Viewpoint, Scope)
An administrative body having the delegated authority to *act* competently as an agent of a higher body. Every *agency* is a *juridical person*, composed of *juridical persons*.

Aggregated records
Activity Model A0/A3: definition of *Authentic, aggregated active records*
Active records which accumulate in interrelated groups according to the way in which a *records creator* carries out its activities.

Analysis of active records
ICOM: A11
See rules in the text of the report related to the activity *SURVEY ACTIVE RECORDS*.

Analysis of inactive records
ICOM: A11
See rules in the text of the report related to the activity *SURVEY INACTIVE RECORDS*.

Analysis of semi-active records
ICOM: A11
See rules in the text of the report related to the activity *SURVEY SEMI-ACTIVE RECORDS*.

ANNOTATE RECORDS
Activity: A3 (A34)
To add to *records* that have already been created.

Annotated records
ICOM: A3
Records that have been added to after their creation, either in the course of handling the matter to which they relate or in the course of their management. Examples of annotations: instructions, dates of hearing or readings, signs beside the text, cross-references, protocol number, classification code, date stamp.

Archival bond
Entity model: as recursive identifying relationship of *Record*
The originary, necessary and determined web of relationships that each *record* has at the moment at which it is made or received with the records that belong in the same aggregation. It is an incremental relationship which begins when a *record* is first connected to another in the course of *action* (e.g., a letter requesting information is linked by an *archival bond* to the draft or copy of the *record* replying to it, and filed with it. The one gives meaning to the other).

Archival documents
Activity Model: Scope
Documents created by a physical or *juridical person* in the course of practical activity. Alias: *records*.

Archival fonds
Activity Model: Title, Purpose
ICOM: A-0/A0
The whole of the *records* created by an *agency* and preserved. Alias: *archives*.

Archival framework
Activity Model: definition of *MANAGE ARCHIVAL FRAMEWORK*
The whole of the policies, rules, instruments, *procedures* and resources (e.g., human, financial), according to which the *records* of an *agency* are managed.

Archival Science
Activity Model (Scope)
ICOM: A-0
The concepts, principles, and methodologies governing the treatment of *records*. It includes the concepts, principles and methodologies defined by *diplomatics*.

Archives
Activity Model: definition of *Archival fonds*
The whole of the *records* created by an *agency* and preserved. Alias: *archival fonds*.

Archives Committee
ICOM: A1
A group of professionals (e.g., records, legal, information technology and services, archival and operational professional experts and managers) with continuing authority for *survey records creator and its records* and *establish archival framework*. Once the *archival framework* is established, the authority for *implementing archival framework* and *maintaining archival framework* passes to the *records office*.

Audit Trail
ICOM A14
An electronic means of auditing all the interactions with *records* within an electronic system so that any access to the system can be documented as it occurs for the purpose of preventing unauthorized *actions* in relation to the *records*, e.g., modification, deletion, or addition, and of ensuring that changes in one of its components do not cause errors elsewhere in the system (the closest correspondent means for the non-electronic components of the *records system* is the charge-out procedure which controls access to *dossiers* and their movement within the *agency*).

Authentic records
Activity Model: definition of *Authentic, aggregated active records*
Records that can be proven to be genuine. Authenticity is conferred on a *record* by its *mode*, *form*, and/or *state of transmission*, and/or manner of preservation and *custody*.

Authentic, aggregated active records
ICOM: A-0/A0/A3
Records which present the characteristics of *authentic records*, *aggregated records*, and *active records*.

Central records system
Activity model: in definition of *CONSIGN RECORDS TO CENTRAL RECORDS SYSTEM*
The central records system is the part of the *records system* that is under the exclusive *competence* of the *records office*.

Changes in administrative and legal context
ICOM: A14
Changes in policies, regulations, and legislation which have occurred since the *integrated business and documentary procedures* were designed and implemented.

CLASS
Entity
The subdivision(s) of a *classification scheme* and the concrete body of *records* corresponding to it (them).

CLASSIFICATION SCHEME
Context entity in entity model
ICOM: A12
Diagram, table, or other representation categorizing the creator's *records* by hierarchical *classes* and according to a coding system expressed in alphabetical, numerical, or alphanumeric symbols. The code associated with each *class* is named the class code.

Classified internal records
ICOM: A2
Internal records that have been classified.

Classified received records
ICOM: A2
Received records that have been classified.

Classified records to be sent
ICOM: A2
Records to be sent that have been classified.

CLASSIFY RECORDS
Activity: A2 (A23)
Assign _records_ to the pre-established _classes_ in the _classification scheme_ and, within each _class_, to the _dossiers_ to which they belong (if applicable), by attaching to each _record_ a classification code.

COMPETENCE
Entity
A sphere of functional responsibility entrusted to an _office_.

COMPETENT ARCHIVAL BODY
Context entity in entity model
Activity Model: definition of _Inactive Records_
The body which is given the exclusive _competence_ for the indefinite preservation of an _agency's inactive records_.

Competent person
Activity Model: definition of _Redirected documents_
The _office_ which is given a _competence_ and has, therefore, the authority and capacity to _act_ within it.

COMPILE RECORDS INVENTORY
Activity: A11 (A115)
The articulation, in a formal _document_, of all the information acquired through the _administrative analysis_, _analysis of inactive records_, _analysis of semi-active records_, and _analysis of active records_, in such a way that the _document_ may be used as the basis for the activity _MANAGE ARCHIVAL FRAMEWORK_.

Completeness
Activity Model: definition of _State of transmission_
The characteristic of _records_ that present all the elements of _physical form_ and _intellectual form_ required by the _agency_ and the _juridical system_.

CONSIGN RECORDS TO CENTRAL RECORDS SYSTEM
Activity: A3 (A31)
Add _records_ to the groups to which they belong, within the _central records system_ , for purposes of reference, use, or subsequent _action_.

CONTINUATIVE ACT
Entity: subtype of *MERE ACT*
An *act* composed of many identical partial *acts* all aimed to the same purpose.

CONTRACT
Entity: subtype of *TRANSACTION*
An *act* accomplished by two or more interacting parties having different motivations and/or interests.

CONVERT RECORDS
Activity: A4 (A43)
To change the *medium* (includes copying to the same kind of *medium*) and/or *physical form* of the *record* in the usual and ordinary course of business (otherwise the activity is not *convert records* but *create records*), leaving intact the *intellectual form*, for purposes of security, disaster prevention, conservation, overcoming technology obsolescence, or compacting the information while preserving the *record's* reliability and authenticity.

Converted records
ICOM: A4
The *records* produced by the activity *CONVERT RECORDS*.

Copied records
ICOM: A3
Records from which one or more copies have been made for business purposes.

Copies of records
ICOM: A0/A3
Reproductions of *records* for business purposes.

COPY RECORDS
Activity: A3(A33)
To make a reproduction of a *record* in any *state of transmission* for business purposes (otherwise it is *CONVERT RECORDS*).

CREATE CLASSIFICATION SCHEME
Activity: A12 (A121)
Develop *classification scheme*.

CREATE RECORDS
Activity: A0/A2
To make and *set aside* or receive and *set aside records*.

CREATE RETENTION SCHEDULE
Activity: A12 (A122)
Develop *retention schedule*.

Creator's holdings
Activity Model: definition of *Inventory of creator's holdings*.
The *records* of a *records creator*.

Creator's mandate and functions
ICOM: A-0
The authority and responsibility given to a *records creator* to administer
predetermined areas of organizational activity, and the way in which such
administration is accomplished.

Custody
Activity Model: definition of *TRANSFER CUSTODY OF INACTIVE RECORDS*
Physical and legal control over the existence, authenticity, location and
accessibility of *records*.

DEFINE ACCESS PRIVILEGES
Activity: A12 (A123)
Determine *access privileges* of specific *officers* according to their *competences*.

DESIGN INTEGRATED BUSINESS AND DOCUMENTARY PROCEDURES
Activity: A13 (A132)
Develop *integrated business and documentary procedures*.

DESIGN RECORDKEEPING AND RECORD-PRESERVATION SYSTEM
Activity: A13 (A131)
Develop *recordkeeping and record-preservation system*.

DESTROY INACTIVE RECORDS
Activity: A4 (A45)
To obliterate *inactive records* from existence without reasonable hope of
recovery.

Destroyed records
ICOM: A4
Inactive records that are obliterated at the time specified in the *retention schedules*.

Diplomatics
Activity Model: definition of *Archival science*
The study of the genesis, inner constitution and transmission of *archival documents*, and of their relationship with the facts represented in them and with their creator.

Document
Entity Model: definition of *Record*.
Information consigned to a *medium*.

DOSSIER
Entity
The smallest interrelated aggregation of *records*, usually named after the person, activity, or subject to which it refers. A *dossier* should not be confused with a *folder*. A *dossier* is a conceptual unit aggregated on the basic of the *action* or matter with which it deals.

ESTABLISH ARCHIVAL FRAMEWORK
Activity: A1 (A12)
To *CREATE CLASSIFICATION SCHEME*, *CREATE RETENTION SCHEDULE* and *DEFINE ACCESS PRIVILEGES*.

Evaluation Report
ICOM: A14
See rules in the text of the report related to the activity *MONITOR RECORDS SYSTEM*.

External initiative
ICOM: A2
An *act*, originating from outside the *agency*, which triggers an *act* within the *agency*.

Facilities
ICOM: A-0
Places where the *records* are stored.

Feedback from Officers
ICOM: A14
See rules in the text of the report related to the activity *MONITOR RECORDS SYSTEM*.

FOLDER
Entity: subtype of *PRESERVATION UNIT*
A cover in which non-electronic *records*, belonging in the same *dossier*, are loosely kept, usually in chronological order. A *dossier* may be distributed across a number of *folders*.

Form
Activity Model: in titles of *physical form* and *intellectual form*.
The *record's physical form* and *intellectual form*.

Form of transmission
Activity Model: definition of *Authentic records*
The *form* that the *record* has when it is received.

FUNCTION
Entity
All of the *acts* aimed to accomplish one purpose within a given jurisdiction or locale.

HANDLE RECORDS
Activity: A0 (A3)
To maintain and use *records* after having consigned them to the *central records system*.

Human Resources
ICOM A-0/A0/A1
People who *manage archival fonds*. They comprise the *archives committee*, the *records office*, the *untrained officers* and the *trained officers*.

IMPLEMENT ARCHIVAL FRAMEWORK
Activity: A1 (A13)
To *DESIGN RECORDKEEPING AND RECORD-PRESERVATION SYSTEM*, *DESIGN INTEGRATED BUSINESS AND DOCUMENTARY PROCEDURES* and *TRAIN OFFICERS*.

Inactive records
Activity model definition of *Accumulation of inactive records*
Records which are no longer needed for ongoing *agency* business.

Incoming documents
ICOM: A-0/A0/A2
Documents received by the *agency* from an external source, including those which the sender already considers *records*.

Information about business procedures
ICOM A1/A12/A13
Information about the *procedures* that define the *actions* and workflow involved in carrying out the *agency's functions*.

Information about records creator
ICOM: A11
See rules in the text of the report related to the activity *SURVEY RECORDS CREATOR*.

Information about records creator and its records
ICOM: A-0/A0/A1/A11
Data concerning the *records creator* and its *records*, obtained from the *records creator* and from its *records* during the activity *SURVEY RECORDS CREATOR AND ITS RECORDS*, and used to produce the *inventory of creator's holdings*.

Information provided by officers
ICOM A11
See rules in the text of the report related to the activity *SURVEY ACTIVE RECORDS*.

Integrated business and documentary procedures
ICOM: A0/A1/A13/A14
Procedures for carrying out the *agency's* business that have been linked to the *records* resulting from each *action* composing them. See rules in the text of the report related to the activity *DESIGN INTEGRATED BUSINESS AND DOCUMENTARY PROCEDURES*.

Integrated classification scheme and retention schedule
ICOM: A1/A12/A13
A recordkeeping instrument which combines and brings into direct relation the *classification scheme* and *retention schedule*.

Intellectual form
Activity Model: definition of *CONVERT RECORDS*
The characteristics of the internal composition of the *record*. It includes content configuration (e.g., text graphics, images), content articulation (elements of the writing and their arrangement), and annotations (additions to the record made after its creation).

INTERNAL RECORD
Entity: subtype of *RECORD*
Records generated within the *agency* and intended for use and dissemination within the *agency* itself. Internal records do not cross the communication boundary between the *agency* and the external world, as established by *agency* policy.

Inventory of creator's holdings
ICOM: A1/A11/A12
A description of the *creator's holdings*, incorporating the results of the *administrative analysis*, the *analysis of inactive records*, the *analysis of semi-active records*, and the *analysis of active records*.

Juridical person
Entity Model: definition of *AGENCY*
An entity having the capacity or potential to *act* legally and constituted either by a collection or succession of natural or physical persons.

Juridical system
ICOM: A-0
A social group organized on the basis of a system of rules. A *juridical system* includes three components: the social group, organizational principle of the social group, and the system of binding rules recognized by the social group (positive law, beliefs, mores, values).

Kept Records
ICOM: A0/A2/A3
Classified internal records, *reliable received records* and *reliable copies of records*.

MAINTAIN ARCHIVAL FRAMEWORK
Activity: A1 (A14)
To *MONITOR RECORDS SYSTEM, REVISE RECORDKEEPING AND RECORD-PRESERVATION SYSTEM, REVISE INTEGRATED BUSINESS AND DOCUMENTARY PROCEDURES*, and *UPDATE OFFICERS*.

MANAGE ARCHIVAL FONDS
Activity: A-0/A0
To control *records* according to the *juridical system;* the *creator's mandate and functions*; and *national and international standards*, using the principles of *archival science*.

MANAGE ARCHIVAL FRAMEWORK
Activity: A0/A1
To *ESTABLISH ARCHIVAL FRAMEWORK, IMPLEMENT ARCHIVAL FRAMEWORK* and *MAINTAIN ARCHIVAL FRAMEWORK*.

Mandate
Activity Model: component of ICOM *Creator's mandate and functions*
The authority and responsibility vested in an *agency* to *act* within a determined area of organizational activity. A *mandate* is exercised by means of *functions*.

Medium
Activity Model: definition of *CONVERT RECORDS*
The material support of the *record* content and *form*. Alias: storage medium.

MEMORANDUM
Entity: Subtype of entity *RECORD*
An *intellectual form* of *record* in which all the persons concurring in the formation of the record appear in the top part of the record. A memorandum is an informal business communication distinguished by the absence of a subscription. In its legal meaning, it is an agreement reached but not yet formally drawn up and signed between the author(s) and the addressee(s).

MERE ACT
Entity: Subtype of entity *ACT*
An *act* which is neither directed toward, nor capable of, changing the relationships between two or more physical or *juridical persons*.

Mode of Transmission
Activity Model: definition of _Authentic records_
The method by which a _record_ is communicated over space or time.

MONITOR RECORDS SYSTEM
Activity Model A14(A141)
Examine the _audit trail_, _protocol register_ and _feedback from officers_ and issue an _evaluation report_.

MULTIPLE ACT
Entity: Subtype of entity _TRANSACTION_
An _act_ accomplished by one physical person or _juridical person_ and directed toward many physical persons or _juridical persons_.

National and international standards
ICOM: A-0
Sets of rules of cooperation among national and international peer entities.

Needed source records
ICOM: A4
Source records after conversion which, instead of being destroyed, are returned to stored _semi-active records_.

OFFICE
Entity
A right and correspondent duty to exercise a trust manifested as a locus for the regular transaction of business or the performance of a given _competence_(s).

Officer
Activity Model: definition of _ACT (n)_
A person holding an _office_.

Officer's initiative
ICOM: A2
An _act_ originating within the _agency_, which triggers another _act_ within the _agency_.

Physical form
Activity Model: definition of _CONVERT RECORDS_

The characteristics of the external appearance of the *record* (e.g., format, colour, configuration, architecture).

PRESERVATION UNIT
Entity
The container in which *records* are placed when they are aggregated.

PRESERVE RECORDS
Activity: A-0/A4
To protect *records* of continuing usefulness. In the course of carrying out this activity, unneeded *records* are destroyed.

PROCEDURE
Entity
The body of written and unwritten rules governing the conduct of an *act*.

PROTOCOL REGISTER
Entity and ICOM A14
A *register* used to assign to *records* a unique, consecutive number and record all the data necessary to identify the persons and *acts* involved and the documentary context of the *record*.

PROTOCOL REGISTER ENTRY
Entity
The entry in the *protocol register* which contains, for every *RECEIVED RECORD* and *SENT RECORD*, a unique, consecutive number and all the data necessary to identify the persons and *acts* involved and the documentary context of the *record*.

RECEIVE DOCUMENTS
Activity: A2 (A22)
To acquire, date-stamp, and *set aside incoming documents*.

RECEIVED RECORD
Entity: subtype of entity *RECORD*
Incoming document that has been *set aside*.

Received records
ICOM: A2
Incoming documents that have been *set aside*.

RECORD
document created by a physical or *juridical person* in the course of practical activity.

RECORDKEEPING AND RECORD-PRESERVATION SYSTEM
Context entity in entity model
A set of internally consistent rules governing recordkeeping, i.e., the making, receiving, setting aside, and handling of *active* and *semi-active records* by the *records creator*, and record-preservation, i.e., the intellectual and physical maintenance of *semi-active* and *inactive records* by the *records creator*, and the *tools* and mechanisms used to implement those rules.

Recordkeeping and record-preservation system
ICOM: A0/A1/A13/A14
A set of internally consistent rules governing recordkeeping, i.e., the making, receiving, setting aside, and handling of *active* and *semi-active records* by the *records creator*, and record-preservation, i.e., the intellectual and physical maintenance of *semi-active* and *inactive records* by the *records creator*, and the *tools* and mechanisms used to implement those rules.

Records
Activity model: Scope
Documents created by a physical or *juridical person* in the course of practical activity. Alias: *archival documents*.

Records' creator
Activity Model: Viewpoint
The physical or *juridical person* who makes, receives, and/or accumulates *records* by reason of its *function*. In this model, the *records' creator* is an *agency*.

Records office
ICOM: A0/A1/A2
The *agency*'s *office*, the exclusive *competences* of which are to carry out the activities *IMPLEMENT ARCHIVAL FRAMEWORK* and *MAINTAIN ARCHIVAL FRAMEWORK* and to oversee the activities *CREATE RECORDS*, *HANDLE RECORDS* , and *PRESERVE RECORDS*.

Records removed from central records system
ICOM: A0/A3/A4

Semi-active records that are no longer needed by the *agency* within the *central records system* but which are still needed for business purposes.

Records system
Activity model: in definition of *CONSIGN RECORDS TO CENTRAL RECORDS SYSTEM*
The system that comprises the *creator's records*, its *recordkeeping and record-preservation system* and is controlled by the creator's records management function.

Records to be consigned to central records system
ICOM: A2
Records which have been made and *set aside* for the purpose of consigning them to the *central records system* but which have not yet been classified.

Records to be sent
ICOM: A2
Records generated within the *agency*, which are intended to cross the communication boundary between the *agency* and the external world.

Redirected documents
ICOM: A2
Documents for which the receiving *agency* or the specific addressee, in his or her capacity as an *officer* of the *agency*, is not the *competent person* and which, therefore, have been returned to the sender or directed to the *competent person*.

REGISTER
Entity: subtype of entity *RECORD*
An *intellectual form* of *record* consisting of blank folios bound together for the regular inclusion of information about *acts*, persons or *records*.

REGISTER RECORDS
Activity: A2 (A24)
Within a *protocol register*, assign to *records* a consecutive number and record all the data necessary to identify the persons and *acts* involved and the documentary context of the *records*.

Reliable copies of sent records
ICOM: A2
Copies of records which have been *registered* and sent.

Reliable received records
ICOM: A2
Received records that have been *registered*.

Reliable sent records
ICOM: A-0/A0/A2
Sent records that have been *registered*.

REMOVE RECORDS FROM CENTRAL RECORDS SYSTEM
Activity: A3 (A35)
Take *semi-active records* out of the *central records system*.

REPORT
Entity: subtype of entity *RECORD*
An *intellectual form* of *record* including a title and a table of contents and used to render an account of, or make a statement about, something heard, seen, done, or researched.

Requests for records
ICOM: A0/A2/A3
A call for *records* by a *records creator*'s *office* or *officer* in order to *act* or to make reference to them.

Retention schedule
Activity Model: definition of *CREATE RETENTION SCHEDULE*
A timetable associated with each *class* of *record*, which determines the retention period, the office of primary responsibility and the final disposition of the *records*.

RETRIEVE RECORDS
Activity: A3 (A32)
To access *records* or remove them from their locations in the *central records system*.

Retrieved records
ICOM: A0/A2/A3
Records that have been accessed or removed from their locations in the *central records system* in order to *act*.

REVIEW RECORDS
Activity: A4
To examine _records_ to determine whether they need to be converted, maintained as they are, transferred, or destroyed.

Reviewed records
ICOM: A4
Records that have been subjected to examination for the purpose of determining whether they need to be converted, maintained as they are, transferred, or destroyed.

REVISE INTEGRATED BUSINESS AND DOCUMENTARY PROCEDURES
Activity A14 (A143)
Modify _integrated business and documentary procedures_ following _changes in administrative and legal context_ and according to _revisions to recordkeeping and record-preservation system_.

REVISE RECORDKEEPING AND RECORD-PRESERVATION SYSTEM
Activity A14 (A142)
Modify _recordkeeping and record-preservation system_ in accordance with the recommendations of the _evaluation report_.

Revisions.to integrated business and documentary procedures
ICOM: A1/A13/A14
Modifications to _integrated business and documentary procedures_ following _changes in administrative and legal context_ and according to _revisions to recordkeeping and record-preservation system_.

Revisions to recordkeeping and record-preservation system
ICOM: A1/A13/A14
Modifications to _recordkeeping and record-preservation system_ in accordance with the recommendations of the _evaluation report_.

Semi-active records
ICOM: A-0/A0/A4
Records which are no longer needed for the purpose of carrying out the _actions_ for which they were created, but which are needed by the _records creator_ for reference.

SENT RECORD
Entity: subtype of entity _RECORD_

A *record* generated within an *agency*, which is intended to cross the communication boundary between the *agency* and the external world.

Set aside
Activity Model: in definition of *CREATE RECORDS*
To retain *records* in order to *act* (i.e., transfer, respond, forward) or for reference.

SIMPLE ACT
Entity: subtype of entity *MERE ACT*
An *act* resulting from one expression of will of a single physical or *juridical person* aimed to one purpose.

Source records after conversion
ICOM: A4
The *records* from which *converted records* have been generated. Among these, those which are still needed for business purposes return to the stored *semi-active records*, while those which are no longer needed for business purposes are destroyed.

State of transmission
Activity Model: definition of *Authentic records*
The primitiveness, *completeness*, and effectiveness of a *record* when it is initially *set aside* after being made or received.

STORE SEMI-ACTIVE RECORDS
Activity: A4 (A41)
To house *records* in office space or off-site according to the frequency of use, retention decisions, and security needs.

SURVEY ACTIVE RECORDS
Activity: A11 (A114)
Examine *active records in offices* and *information provided by officers* in light of the *administrative analysis*, the *analysis of inactive records* and the *analysis of semi-active records*, in order to produce an *analysis of active records*.

SURVEY INACTIVE RECORDS
Activity: A11 (A112)
Examine *accumulation of inactive records* in light of the *administrative analysis* in order to produce an *analysis of inactive records*.

SURVEY RECORDS CREATOR
Activity: A11 (A111)
Examine the *information about records creator* in order to produce an *administrative analysis*.

SURVEY RECORDS CREATOR AND ITS RECORDS
Activity: A1 (A11)
To design and enact a methodology for collecting, compiling and analyzing data about the *records creator* and its *records*.

SURVEY SEMI-ACTIVE RECORDS
Activity: A11 (A113)
Examine *accumulation of semi-active records* in light of the *administrative analysis* and the *analysis of inactive records* in order to produce an *analysis of semi-active records*

Tools
ICOM: A-0
Hardware, software and other equipment and supplies used to generate, transmit, manage, and store *records*.

Trained officers
ICOM: A0/A1/A13/A14
Management *officers*, action *officers*, and records *officers* who have undergone training associated with the activity *IMPLEMENT ARCHIVAL FRAMEWORK*.

TRAIN OFFICERS
Activity: A13 (A133)
To familiarize *officers* of the *agency* with the *recordkeeping and record-preservation system* and instruct them on the *integrated business and documentary procedures*.

TRANSACTION
Entity: subtype of entity *ACT*
An *act* capable of changing the relationship between two or more physical or *juridical persons*.

TRANSFER CUSTODY OF INACTIVE RECORDS
Activity: A4 (A44)
To physically and legally pass *custody* of *inactive records* to the *competent archival body*.

Transferred inactive records
ICOM: A-0/A0/A4
Inactive records, the *custody* of which has been passed to a *competent archival body*.

Untrained officers
ICOM: A1/A13
Officers who have not yet undergone training associated with the activity *IMPLEMENT ARCHIVAL FRAMEWORK*.

UPDATE OFFICERS
Activity A14 (A144)
Familiarize *trained officers* with *revisions to recordkeeping and record-preservation system* and instruct them on *revisions to the integrated business and documentary procedures*.

Updated officers
ICOM: A1/A14
Trained officers who have been familiarized with *revisions to recordkeeping and record-preservation system* and instructed on *revisions to the integrated business and documentary procedures*.

VOLUME
Entity: subtype of entity *PRESERVATION UNIT*
An aggregation of *records* bound together physically by the creating *office* for purposes of maintenance and use. The *records* usually relate to the same subject, derive from the same activity, and/or are arranged in chronological order.

Appendix D
Procedural Rules for Managing an Agency's Archival Fonds

Procedural rules have been written for the MANAGE ARCHIVAL FRAMEWORK activities that appear on diagrams A11, A12, A13, and A14, the CREATE RECORDS activities that appear on diagram A2, the HANDLE RECORDS activities that appear on diagram A3, and the PRESERVE RECORDS activities that appear on diagram A4. The procedural rules are intended to provide guidance to managers within agencies who have responsibility for establishing procedures for managing the agency's archival fonds and for determining the design requirements for an electronic recordkeeping system.

RULES FOR ACTIVITIES INVOLVED IN MANAGE ARCHIVAL FRAMEWORK

RULE A111
SURVEY RECORDS CREATOR

To survey records creator, construct an administrative analysis in accordance with the following rules:

a) if records creator is a public body, then search information about records creator for legislative authority, mandate, functions, business procedures, structure and how these have evolved over time, and, on the basis of this, write an administrative analysis;

b) if records creator is a private body, then search information about records creator for articles of incorporation, mission, functions, business procedures, structure and how these have evolved over time, and, on the basis of this, write an administrative analysis.

RULE A112 SURVEY INACTIVE RECORDS

To survey inactive records, construct an analysis of inactive records in accordance with the following rules:

a) if there are inactive records kept by the records creator, then write an analysis of inactive records, describing the following:

1. the current identifier of each aggregate of inactive records, its nature and purpose, medium and form, inclusive dates, physical extent, relationships with other aggregations, and arrangement;
2. existing control instruments (lists, schedules, indexes, cross references, etc.);
3. office of primary responsibility;
4. location;
5. retention needs;
6. access needs;
7. relationship to the administrative analysis;

b) if there are inactive records of the records creator kept by a competent archival body, or by the office of primary responsibility, then analyze 1 and 2 and write an analysis of inactive records.

RULE A113
SURVEY SEMI-ACTIVE RECORDS

To survey semi-active records, construct an analysis of semi-active records in accordance with the following rules.

For each aggregate of semi-active records, write an analysis describing the following:

1. the current identifier of the records, their nature and purpose, medium and form, inclusive dates, physical extent, relationships with other aggregations, and arrangement;
2. existing control instruments (lists, schedules, indexes, cross references, etc.);
3. office of primary responsibility;
4. type and frequency of use;
5. rate of accumulation;
6. location;
7. retention needs;
8. access needs;
9. relationship to the administrative analysis.

RULE A114
SURVEY ACTIVE RECORDS

To survey active records, construct an analysis of active records in accordance with the following rules.

For each office of the records creator write an analysis of active records describing the following for each aggregate:

1. the current identifier of the group of records, its nature and purpose, medium and form, inclusive dates, physical extent, relationships with other aggregations, and arrangement;
2. existing control instruments (lists, schedules, indexes, cross-references, etc.);
3. competent office;
4. rate of accumulation;
5. location;
6. retention needs;
7. access needs;
8. relationship to the administrative analysis.

RULE A115
COMPILE RECORDS INVENTORY

Compile an inventory of creator's holdings in accordance with the following rules:

a) compare the analyses of the inactive, semi-active, and active records to identify the similarities and differences; then combine the analyses to eliminate redundancy;

b) draft inventory of creator's holdings on the basis of the analysis;

c) review inventory with officers of records creator for the purpose of identifying and verifying retention periods and access needs; and

d) issue inventory.

A121
CREATE CLASSIFICATION SCHEME

Review inventory of creator's holdings and relate to information about business procedures to create a classification scheme by:

a) identifying hierarchical classes of records in terms of agency functions, procedures and acts;

b) naming the hierarchical classes;

c) describing the scope of each hierarchical class and the arrangement of the records and/or dossiers within it; and

d) selecting coding scheme and expressing class relationships in terms of coding scheme.

A122
CREATE RETENTION SCHEDULE

Create a retention schedule and integrate it with the classification scheme in accordance with the following rules:

a) review the classification scheme, the inventory of creator's holdings, and the information about business procedures in order to define the active, semi-active and inactive periods of retention[1] of the classes of records, and the medium and place of their retention, by:

1. identifying how long records of each class are needed for business purposes;
2. identifying the medium in which they need to be retained based on frequency of use, location of use, reference time, and retrieval time;[2]
3. identifying the legal retention requirements for each class of records (per statutes and regulations);
4. identifying classes of records which should be retained indefinitely;
5. associating each class of record with an Office of Primary Responsibility[3] (OPR) that will have responsibility for the retention of the original records; and
6. establishing distinct retention periods by class for copies of non-electronic records existing in different offices than the OPR;

b) integrate resulting retention periods with the classification scheme by linking them to the class to which they refer.

A123
DEFINE ACCESS PRIVILEGES

Define access privileges in accordance with the following rules:

a) establish the general access rule (either open or restricted access for retrieval and viewing) and then specify the exceptions;

b) prohibit the modification[4] of records once they have been classified;

c) assign access privileges to offices/officers for each class of records on the basis of their competence;

d) allow the office/officer that creates the records unrestricted access to them;

e) allow the handling office/officer[5] and the records office/officer to annotate records;

f) allow access to the records by the records office/officer for the purpose of classification; and

g) give the records office/officer exclusive authority to access the records for purposes of transfer or destruction.

A131
DESIGN RECORDKEEPING AND RECORD-PRESERVATION SYSTEM

Design a recordkeeping and record-preservation system in accordance with the following rules:

a) establish that the recordkeeping and record-preservation system will control all the records of the agency, both electronic and non-electronic;

b) establish that the integrated control of the records will take place within the electronic system;

c) define, within the electronic system, boundaries of general, group and individual space as follows:

1. the boundaries of the individual space coincide with the jurisdiction of the officer to whom it is assigned by the agency. The address of the individual space includes the formal title of the office/officer. If the agency wishes, it may assign a personal space to each employee, along with an address corresponding to his or her personal name, for his or her own private use (e.g., subscriptions to listservs, informal correspondence with fellow employees). If the individual space is linked to competence it could allow for the routine carrying out of certain procedures (according to workflow rules);
2. the boundaries of group space coincide with the jurisdiction of the office/program/team/committee/working group, etc. to which a specific competence/charge/responsibility/task etc. has been assigned by the agency. The address of the group space includes the name of the group;
3. the boundaries of general space coincide with the jurisdiction of the records office which is responsible for the records system of the agency. The address of the general space is the address of the agency

d) determine, on the basis of the above-mentioned boundaries:

1. the space in which records are made;

2. the space in which records are received;
3. the space in which records may be revised, modified or otherwise altered;
4. the space in which records can be individually destroyed;
5. the space in which records will be classified;
6. the space in which records will be registered;
7. the space in which originals are stored;
8. the space in which the retention schedule is implemented; and
9. the right of access to each space, based on access privileges

e) assign exclusive competence to the records office for the classification, profiling, registration, and consignment to the central records system of all the incoming and outgoing non-electronic records;

f) assign exclusive competence to the records office for the classification, profiling, and consignment to the central records system of all internal non-electronic records;

g) define rules by which electronic records move inside and outside the agency by determining:

1. what are the components of the record profile for incoming, outgoing and internal records in accordance with their state of transmission and the space to which they are communicated;[6]
2. the routing of the records received by the agency and sent by the agency (determining whether records can be received from outside the agency directly into the individual space or sent directly from the individual space to outside the agency);[7] and
3. the possibility of generating common work spaces, not only within the agency, but, also, across agencies, and establishing routines related to them;

h) establish the routine according to which the electronic system will generate a record profile form[8] in connection with each record.[9] The profile will serve the purpose of an annotation and be linked inextricably to the record;[10]

i) design a record profile form that includes the following fields:[11]

- protocol number[12]
- date of receipt[13]
- time of receipt[14]
- date of transmission[15]
- time of transmission[16]
- date of record[17]
- archival date[18]
- protocol number of sending office[19]
- originator's name[20]
- originator's address[21]
- author's name[22]

- author's address[23]
- writer's name[24]
- writer's address[25]
- action or matter[26]
- number of attachments[27]
- medium[28]
- handling office[29]
- action taken[30]
- addressee's name[31]
- addressee's address[32]
- receiver's name[33]
- receiver's address[34]
- class code[35]
- dossier identifier[36]
- record item identifier[37]
- mode of transmission[38]
- draft number;[39]

j) define the required fields of the record profile for each record within the electronic system. The research team recommends the following:

1. every record made in the individual space, in order to be saved in that space, must include in its record profile at least:
    - date of record,
    - author,
    - addressee,
    - action or matter;
2. every record made in the individual space, in order to be transmitted to another individual space or to the group space, must include in its record profile, in addition to the elements identified in (1): date and time of transmission, receiver(s), number of attachments, class code and dossier identifier (if applicable);
3. every record made in the individual space, in order to be transmitted to the general space, must include in its record profile all the elements identified in the list in (i) with the following exceptions:
    - in the case of originator and writer, if they are inapplicable (because they are identical to the author) these fields may be left empty;
    - the protocol number, which will be added in the general space by the system for outgoing records;
    - the record item identifier which will be added in the general space by the system;
4. every incoming record received in the individual space from the general space, in order to be consigned to the central records system, must include in its record profile all the elements identified in the list in (i) with the following exceptions:

- in the case of originator and writer, if they are inapplicable (because they are identical to the author) these fields may be left empty;
- the record item identifier which will be added in the general space by the system;

5. every record made in the group space, in order to be saved and/or transmitted within the group space, must include in its record profile, in addition to the elements identified in (1), the names of receivers, the number of attachments, the draft number and the class code and dossier identifier;

6. every record made in the group space, in order to be transmitted to the individual space, must include in its record profile all the elements identified in (1) and (2);

7. every record made in the group space, in order to be transmitted to the general space, must include in its record profile, all the elements identified in (3);

8. no record can be made in the general space;

9. every record received in the general space from outside the agency which is not addressed to a specific office or officer, must include in its record profile, all the elements identified in the list in (i);

10. no record can be transmitted from the general space to the individual or group space other than by copying it with its record profile attached;[40]

11. all outgoing electronic records are transmitted from the general space to the outside after a copy has been made and consigned, with the record profile, to the central records system;

k) define the required fields for the record profile for each non-electronic record that is consigned to the central records system.[41] The research team recommends the following, as applicable:

- protocol number
- date of receipt
- date of record
- archival date
- protocol number of sending office
- author's name
- author's address
- writer's name
- writer's address
- action or matter
- number of attachments
- medium
- handling office
- action taken
- addressee's name
- addressee's address
- receiver's name
- receiver's address

- class code
- dossier identifier
- record item identifier
- draft number

l) establish procedures for registration which determine:

1. whether certain types of internal records will be registered and what types of internal records will be registered;
2. who will be responsible for registering the records;
3. when the records will be registered;
4. where the data to be recorded in the register are to be taken from;[42]
5. what data is to be recorded in the register;[43]
6. the time span of the register;[44]
7. the access privileges for the register;
8. the classification code to be assigned to the register and the retention requirements associated with it;

m) establish status of transmission[45] of electronic records (original,[46] draft,[47] copy[48])and draft control as follows:

1. Any record that has not been transmitted is a draft;[49]
2. Any record transmitted to the general space is received as an original;
3. Any record transmitted externally is consigned to the central record system of the sender as a copy of the last draft and received by the addressee as an original;
4. Any record received from outside the agency is received as an original;
5. Every record received in the group space is received as an original but can be altered and transformed into a draft of another record;
6. Every comment on drafts received in the group space is an original and must be capable of being linked to the draft to which it relates;
7. The sequence of the various drafts of the same record circulating in the group and individual spaces must be numbered;

n) establish methods and rules for authentication of records by:

1. linking to the integrated business and documentary procedures the authentication requirements for specific types of records and assigning responsibility to officers/offices for implementing the requirements;
2. assigning to the records office the competence for authenticating copies of records which reside within the central records system;
3. establishing the authentication procedure for each form of conversion of records;
4. identifying the method of authentication for every record medium; and
5. creating a final view of the records profiles of all the records within a dossier or class before removing it from the central records system as instructed in q(5);

o) establish methods and rules for protecting confidentiality by:

identifying confidential classes of records;
identifying the method for protecting confidentiality for every record medium;
assigning responsibility for implementing the methods and rules; and
identifying methods of ensuring confidentiality of transmissions within and outside
    the agency;

p) establish rules for copying by:

1. identifying the need for generating records in multiple copies in any medium
    on the exclusive basis of working needs and vital records needs;
2. identifying the various types of copies (e.g., simple transcription, imitative
    copy, copy in the form of original, authentic copy, insert) and the authority to
    be accorded to each type; and
3. establishing procedures for routine copying of records which are needed
    beyond the life expectancy of their medium;

q) establish an electronic method of showing the connection among active
records in all media which belong in the same aggregation by:

1. recording in the electronic system the location of non-electronic records
    belonging in the same aggregation as the electronic records in the system;
2. establishing an electronic link which allows for a complete view of the
    descriptions[50] of the records -- and of their individual profile if needed -- in the
    dossier or class regardless of their media;
3. establishing a system which allows access to these views by class;
4. in the case of ongoing dossiers that are routinely closed on an annual
    basis,[51] establishing the capability to retain a complete view of the
    descriptions of the records that have been removed from the central records
    system;
5. creating a final view of the record profiles of all the records in each dossier
    before it is removed from the central records system[52];
6. removing each closed dossier, along with the final view of its records profiles,
    from the central records system;

r) establish a tracking and location system by:

1. instituting charge-out procedures for all the records preservation units (e.g.,
    folder, volume, tape, disk) which are not contained within the electronic
    system;
2. when a closed dossier is removed from the system, assigning a location
    which is recorded within the electronic system according to class;[53] and
3. establishing a procedure for maintaining up-to-date location information for
    all active and semi-active records in all media;

s) establish a retrieval system for active and semi-active records by:

1. developing a thesaurus to the classification scheme[54] and linking the thesaural descriptors to the class codes to allow for the searching of records by those descriptors;
2. instituting a procedure for indexing the records using descriptors drawn from the thesaurus;
3. indexing all the fields of the record profile;
4. building in the capability, within the group and individual spaces, of searching records by class code and keyword; and
5. determining the means of retrieving information from the protocol register;

t) establish audit procedures by:

1. maintaining an audit trail of access to the records system to control the administration and use of access privileges; and
2. maintaining an audit trail of every transmission (date, time, persons, action or matter) within the records system;

u) establish procedures to prevent loss or corruption of records because of intentional or inadvertent unauthorized additions, deletions, or alterations by:

1. providing the electronic system with the capability to restrict access to the backup procedures to authorized personnel;
2. prescribing that backup copies of records and their profiles be made periodically;[55]
3. maintaining an audit trail of additions and changes to records since the last periodic backup. It should contain the information necessary to provide recovery of records in the event of system failure and it should be maintained on an electronic system different from the one containing the records;
4. maintaining a system backup that includes system programs, operating system files, etc.;
5. maintaining at least three periodic backups. The oldest backup copy should be deleted upon successful creation of a new backup copy. Any audits earlier than the oldest backup copy should be deleted;
6. ensuring that, following any system failure, the backup and recovery procedures will automatically guarantee that all complete updates (records and any control information such as indexes required to access the records) contained in the audit are reflected in the rebuilt files and will also guarantee that any incomplete operation is backed up. The capability should be provided to rebuild forward from any backup copy, using the backup copy and all subsequent audit trails;[56]

v) establish procedures to prevent the loss of records due to factors such as technological obsolescence (of hardware, system software, and storage media such as: storage devices, access methods, and database management systems) by:

1. planning upgrades to the agency's recordkeeping technology base;

2. ensuring the ability to retrieve and use stored records when components of the electronic system are changed; and
3. migrating records;

w) establish procedure for taking records out of the central records system for preservation purposes by:

1. identifying the officers authorized to remove records from the system;
2. determining storage medium and location for records removed from the system;
3. determining what has to be removed along with the records (e.g., indexes, data directories, data dictionaries, profiles, register entries, etc.);
4. using the retention schedule to implement the transition of records from active to semi-active status and from semi-active to inactive status; and
5. determining methods of transfer of inactive records from the agency to the competent archival body and the form in which the records will be transferred;

x) establish records storage facilities and equipment requirements by:

1. forecasting rate of accumulation of active and semi-active records by medium;
2. determining space and climate control requirements; and
3. determining the need for records storage facilities and equipment (filing cabinets, records servers, etc.);

y) determine requirements for the electronic component of the recordkeeping system by identifying:

1. functional requirements;
2. national and international documentation and communication standards;
3. metadata of the electronic system;[57]
4. office applications and communication software to be used to create, handle and preserve records; and
5. interoperability requirements of office applications, communication software, and recordkeeping software;

z) Compile all recordkeeping policies.

A132
DESIGN INTEGRATED BUSINESS AND DOCUMENTARY PROCEDURES

Design integrated business and documentary procedures in accordance with the following rules:

a) identify all the business procedures within each function;

b) determine, for each procedure,[58] whether the procedure is constitutive,[59] executive,[60] instrumental[61] or organizational;[62]

c) for each procedure within each function, break down procedure into the 6 phases of a procedure,
i.e.,

* initiative[63]
* inquiry[64]
* consultation[65]
* deliberation[66]
* deliberation control[67]
* execution[68]

d) determine, for each phase of each procedure:

1.   the component actions;
2.   the records that must be used in relation to each action;[69]
3.   the records that must be made, received, and handled in the course of each action[70] and by whom;
4.   how the records are to be classified, audited, and disposed;
5.   the level of confidentiality of the records; and
6.   the methods for ensuring their reliability and authenticity;

e) establish a directory of competences and access privileges

---

A133
TRAIN OFFICERS

The procedural rules governing this activity have not been developed since such procedures are specific to each agency.

A141
MONITOR RECORDS SYSTEM

To monitor records system, prepare an evaluation report in accordance with the following process:

a) obtain feedback from officers in accordance with pre-established procedures;

b) determine compliance of offices/officers with recordkeeping and record-preservation rules, e.g., profiling, registration, classification, retention, conversion;

c) evaluate adequacy of storage facilities and equipment;

d) evaluate adequacy of system backup and recovery procedures;

e) identify changes in legal context, business procedures, classes of records, office of primary responsibility for classes of records;

f) identify changes in retention requirements for existing classes of records;

g) determine retention periods for new classes of records;

h) evaluate the impact of technological change on recordkeeping and record-preservation; and

i) produce an evaluation report describing findings

A142
REVISE RECORDKEEPING AND RECORD-PRESERVATION SYSTEM

Revise recordkeeping and record-preservation system in accordance with the following guideline:

a) for each item in the evaluation report related to the recordkeeping and record-preservation system, and which indicates a need for change:

1. determine the modifications needed; and
2. implement them.

A143
REVISE INTEGRATED BUSINESS AND DOCUMENTARY PROCEDURES

Revise integrated business and documentary procedures in accordance with the following guidelines:

a) determine the impact of changes (if any) in the administrative and legal context on the integrated business and documentary procedures, e.g., changes in phases, actions; intellectual form of the records, office competent for making, receiving, or handling the records; and

b) for each change, revise the integrated business and documentary procedures

A144
UPDATE OFFICERS

The procedural rules governing this activity have not been developed since they are specific to each agency.

RULES FOR ACTIVITIES INVOLVED IN CREATE RECORDS, HANDLE RECORDS, AND PRESERVE RECORDS

RULE A21
ACT

The procedural rules governing the activity to ACT are:

a) if act consists of, and requires, producing a document, then set aside the dispositive record[71] by filling in the required elements of the record profile according to the space in which the record is being saved or transmitted to;

b) if act does not consist of producing a document, but requires a document, then make document[72] and set aside the probative record[73] by filling in the required elements of the record profile according to the space in which the record is being saved or transmitted to;

c) if a document provides support to act, then make document and set aside the supporting record[74] by filling in the required elements of the record profile according to the space in which the record is being saved or transmitted to;

d) if act is oral and a document is not required, but a document is wanted for memory, then make document and set aside the narrative record[75]by filling in the required elements of the record profile according to the space in which the record is being saved or transmitted to; and

e) if act requires consulting record(s) already consigned to the central records system, then request record(s).[76]

RULE A22
RECEIVE DOCUMENTS

The procedural rules governing the activity RECEIVE DOCUMENTS are as follows:

a) if agency is competent, then records office or officer date-stamps and sets aside record by:

1. in the case of an incoming electronic record which is not addressed to a specific office or officer, filling in the record profile, forwarding the record, with its profile, to the competent office or officer, and consigning to the central records system a copy of the record along with its record profile;
2. in the case of an incoming electronic record which is addressed to a specific office or officer, if the addressees' e-mail address is that of the office/officer who has to handle the matter, letting the system use its capability of forwarding the record directly to it after having assigned to the record the protocol number and the date of receipt; the addressee will then fill in the record profile and consign the record, along with the record profile, to the central records system;
3. in the case of a non-electronic record, filling in the record profile within the electronic general space, copying on the original record its classification code and protocol number and forwarding it to the competent office or officer;

else:

b) if another agency is competent, then the records office or officer redirects document as follows:

1. if the redirected document is electronic and the protocol number has been automatically generated, record in the profile entry field, "Action taken," the word "Redirected." By default, the only other fields of the record profile that will be filled in are the author, the addressee, the date of receipt, and the action or matter;
2. if the redirected document is non-electronic, generate a record profile form, assign a protocol number and record in the profile entry field, "Action taken," the word "Redirected." By default, the only other fields of the record profile that will be filled in are the author, the addressee, the date of receipt, and the action or matter;
3. if the specific addressee is competent, but not in his or her capacity as an officer of the agency, then, redirect document as specified above;
4. if another competence is not identifiable, then, return document to sender as specified in (b) (1) and (2), but substitute "Returned" for "Redirected" in the "Action taken" field of the record profile;
5. if incoming document is ephemeral (e.g., junk mail), then, follow the same process as described in (b) (1) and (2), but substitute "Ephemera--

disposed" for "Redirected" in the "Action taken" field of the record profile and dispose of incoming document.[77]

RULE A23
CLASSIFY RECORDS

Classify records in accordance with the following rules:

a) determine the appropriate class code and dossier identifier of the record by searching the classification scheme, through its thesaurus and the repertory of dossiers and record the data in the record profile;[78]

b) if a dossier has not yet been opened on the action or matter to which the record pertains, then, open a new dossier and enter it into the repertory of dossiers.[79]

RULE A24
REGISTER RECORDS

Register incoming and outgoing records in accordance with the following rules:

a) all incoming and outgoing records, in electronic and non-electronic form, are assigned a symbol specifying whether they are incoming or outgoing (in the case of non-electronic records, this symbol is added manually either to the electronic record profile or to the electronic copy of the scanned document);

b) a record profile is prepared for each incoming and outgoing record. The records presenting the incoming or outgoing symbol will automatically be registered by extracting from the record profile the pertinent data (e.g., outgoing records would not have date of receipt filled in);

c) if action taken is simply to consign to the central records system the incoming record, then enter the words "consigned to central records system" in the action taken field of the record profile for the incoming record;

d) if the action taken is a material action, then enter a description of the material action in the action taken field of the record profile for the incoming record;

e) an incoming non-electronic record is date stamped as soon as it arrives and is assigned a classification code which is inscribed within the date stamp. Then the record office generates in the electronic system a record profile to which the system assigns a protocol number. The data in the profile become the register entry and the protocol number is manually transcribed by the record office within the date stamp on the record;

f) an incoming electronic record is first assigned a protocol number within the general space. A register entry will not be completed for the record until its record profile has been completed by the handling office (which might be the records office).[80]

RULE A31
CONSIGN RECORDS TO CENTRAL RECORDS SYSTEM

Consign records to the central records system in accordance with the following rules:

a) establish that a record will be consigned to the central records system only when authorized by a competent records officer;

b) establish that every kept record will be entered in the central records system according to its classification code;

c) establish that every received record will be entered in the central records system according to its classification code before it is handed to the officer competent for handling the matter;

d) if the record medium is paper then place the record at the beginning of the file folder corresponding to the appropriate classification code;

e) establish procedures for assigning to each record a unique record item identifier;[81]

f) establish procedures for assigning to each record an archival date[82] when the record receives its record item identifier;

g) establish that every kept non-electronic record that has been retrieved will be returned to the central records system unless it is being retrieved for the purpose of removing it from the central records system in accordance with the retention schedule;

h) establish that any retrieved non-electronic record which is returned to the central records system will be refiled in the same position from which it was retrieved;

i) prohibit the placing of multiple copies of the same record as consecutive items in the same dossier;

j) establish that annotated records will be reconsigned to the central records system without creating a new profile.

RULE A32
RETRIEVE RECORDS

Retrieve records from the central records system in accordance with the following rules:

a) establish that the records office has exclusive competence for retrieving non-electronic records from the central records system, based on the access privileges of the requester;

b) establish that the system will retrieve electronic records from the central records system based on the access privileges of the requester;[83]

c) establish that the system will retrieve electronic records and the profiles of non-electronic records according to the fields of the record profile and the descriptors drawn from the thesaurus;

d) establish that the system and/or the records office will retrieve the entire record, including all annotations and attachments;

e) establish that, when a record that is requested is part of a dossier, the entire dossier will be retrieved.

RULE A33
COPY RECORDS

Copy records in accordance with the following rules:

a) establish that the records office has exclusive competence for copying non-electronic records stored in the central records system;

b) establish that the system or the records office will be able to produce simple,[84] imitative[85] and authentic[86] copies;

c) establish that a simple copy cannot be used as an authoritative or authentic copy;

d) establish that an authentic copy will be required to satisfy external requests for records;

e) establish that an imitative authentic copy will be the only type of copy used for preservation purposes;

f) establish that records office has exclusive competence for making authentic copies of the records in the central records system.

g) establish that the records office has exclusive competence for the routine copying of the records in the system made for preservation, for security reasons, or for satisfying external requests. The resulting copies will be accorded the same authority as authentic copies because of the controls on the reproduction process.

RULE A34
ANNOTATE RECORDS

Annotate records in accordance with the following rules:

a) establish that each annotation will bear identification of the officer annotating and the date of the annotation;

b) establish that an annotation will be inextricably bound to the record;

c) establish that a copy made to replace a record for reasons of preservation will be annotated before being reconsigned to the central records system by indicating in the profile the date of copying and the fact that the original has been destroyed;

d) establish that only the office or officer competent for the action in which the record participates is permitted to annotate a record vis a vis execution and/or handling of the action or matter;

e) establish that the records office has exclusive competence for annotating a record for records management purposes.

RULE A35
REMOVE RECORDS FROM CENTRAL RECORDS SYSTEM[87]

Remove records from the central records system in accordance with the following rules:

a) establish that the records office has the exclusive competence to remove records from the central records system;

b) establish that, if the retention schedule indicates that dossiers or individual records within a class have reached the end of their active retention period, and the records office has received authorization from the office of primary responsibility to apply the retention rule to them, then, the records office will remove the records from the central records system, along with their corresponding profiles. Authorization for removal of all or part of the records in question cannot be withheld unless a compelling and tangible reason for doing so is presented, along with a proposed new date of removal;

c) establish that, when the dossiers or individual records are to be removed from the central records system to be transferred to semi-active storage or to the competent archival body, an annotation indicating the medium on which they are being transferred and the date of removal will be added to the profile;

d) establish that, when the dossiers are to be removed from the central records system to be transferred to semi-active storage or to the competent archival body, a final view of the dossiers' profiles will be generated, a copy of which will remain in the general space of the electronic system while the other copy accompanies the dossier. In the case of non-electronic records, the profiles for each dossier will be printed out and attached to the dossier;

e) establish that, when the dossiers or individual records are removed from the central records system to be destroyed, their corresponding profiles are destroyed also;

f) establish that, when the dossiers or individual records are to be removed from the central records system to be transferred or destroyed, their corresponding entry in the protocol register will remain in the system for as long as the retention period for the protocol register requires;

g) establish that protocol registers will be removed from the central records system and transferred to semi-active storage on an annual basis at the end of each calendar or fiscal year.

RULE A41
STORE SEMI-ACTIVE RECORDS

Store semi-active records in accordance with the following rules:

a) establish that the records office has exclusive competence for managing the records in the semi-active storage location and for retrieving them from and returning them to that location;

b) establish that, when semi-active records are retrieved from the semi-active storage location for business reasons, they will only be reconsigned to the central records system if they are formally reactivated. Formal reactivation applies only to dossiers and derives solely from the creation of additional records for a dossier stemming from a resurrection of the action or matter. Otherwise, the semi-active records are to be returned to the semi-active storage location.

RULE A42
REVIEW RECORDS

Review records in accordance with the following rules:

a) establish that the records office has the exclusive competence to review records;

b) establish that the records office will periodically examine the records in semi-active storage to determine whether they need to be converted or maintained as they are;

c) establish that, when the retention schedule indicates the records have reached the end of their semi-active period, the records office will review the records for the purpose of obtaining authorization from the office of primary responsibility to transfer custody of the inactive records to the competent archival body or destroy them. Authorization for transfer of all or part of the records in question cannot be withheld unless a compelling and tangible reason for doing so is presented, along with a proposed new date of transfer;

d) establish that, if the records office determines that the reviewed records need to be converted, then it will select the medium and physical form.

RULE A43
CONVERT RECORDS

Convert records in accordance with the following rules:

a) establish that the records office has the exclusive competence to convert records;

b) establish that, if the converted records are destined for transfer to the competent archival body, the source records after conversion will be returned to the semi-active records storage location if still needed by the agency or destroyed if they are no longer needed;

c) establish that, if records are converted because of deterioration or obsolescence, then, the source records after conversion will be destroyed;

d) establish that, before destroying any source records after conversion, the records office will ensure that the converted records are capable of being read;

e) establish that an indication of the new medium and physical form, along with the date of conversion, will be attached to the records profile of each converted record as an annotation.

RULE A44
TRANSFER CUSTODY OF INACTIVE RECORDS

Transfer custody of inactive records in accordance with the following rules:

a) establish that the records office has exclusive competence for transferring custody of inactive records to the competent archival body;

b) establish that the records office will transfer dossiers or individual records belonging to a class only in accordance with the established records schedule and only after having obtained authorization from the office of primary responsibility. Authorization for transfer of all or part of the records in question cannot be withheld unless a compelling and tangible reason for doing so is presented, along with a proposed new date of transfer;

c) establish that, when the dossiers are to be transferred to the competent archival body, a final view of the dossiers' profiles, including a final annotation indicating the date of transfer, will be generated and will accompany the dossiers (as an electronic file in the case of electronic records and as a printout in the case of non-electronic records) as a form of authentication of the dossiers;

d) establish that, when inactive records are transferred to the competent archival body, the final view of the dossiers, which may have been annotated during the records' semi-active period, will be removed from the agency's records system, along with the dossiers.

RULE A45
DESTROY INACTIVE RECORDS

Destroy inactive records in accordance with the following rules:

a) establish that the records office has exclusive competence for destroying inactive records;

b) establish that the records office will determine the appropriate method of destruction, depending on the medium and degree of sensitivity of the records;

c) establish that the records will be obliterated from existence without any reasonable hope of recovery;

d) establish that the records office will destroy dossiers or individual records in accordance with the retention schedule after having obtained authorization from the office of primary responsibility. Authorization for destruction of all or part of the records in question cannot be withheld unless a compelling and tangible reason for doing so is presented, along with a proposed new date of destruction; and

e) establish that, when dossiers are destroyed, the final views of their profiles which have remained in the central records system will be destroyed along with them.[88]

Endnotes

[1] The status of a class of records as active or inactive is often equated, mistakenly, with the status of its component dossiers as open or closed. It should be pointed out that the level of activity of a class of records relates purely to the frequency of use of the records in relation to business purposes, while the closure of dossiers, or of folders within dossiers, is linked, respectively, to the closure of the matter to which the dossier relates, and to the physical management needs of the preservation unit(s) composing the dossier or series (e.g., folders or volumes). Dossiers may be, at the same time, open and semi-active or inactive because, while the matter to which they relate is not concluded, their frequency of use falls below an established rate. By the same token, dossiers may be closed but still retain a semiactive status because they still need to be consulted for business purposes. Furthermore, a dossier may remain open while its component parts (e.g., the individual folders composing it) are regularly closed for management reasons (e.g., at the end of each fiscal year).

[2] Frequency of use refers to the number of times within a determined time span that a record needs to be retrieved for use by the competent office/officer; location of use refers to the place(s) where a given type of record needs to be consulted; reference time refers to the amount of uninterrupted time the competent office/officer needs to consult a given type of record; retrieval time refers to the amount of time it takes to retrieve the specific record required by the competent office/officer.

[3] The office of primary responsibility is the office to which is given formal competence for the preserve records activity for a given class of records within the integrated classification scheme and retention schedule.

[4] Modification of a record means a change to its content, content articulation or content configuration. Any annotation which is added to the record, either in the course of handling it or in the course of managing it is not to be considered a modification. In the case of electronic forms, the filling in of the form constitutes the making of a record not a modification of it. Once all the required fields have been filled in, the form may be treated as an entity which should not be modified. It remains understood that, once a field has been filled in, it should not be modifiable.

[5] The handling office/officer is the office or officer which is formally competent for carrying out the action to which the record relates or for the matter to which the record pertains.

[6] Communication can take place over time or through space. Communication over time occurs when a record is saved in the same space in which it was made, in order to return to it at a later time. Communication through space occurs when a record is transmitted from one person to another.

[7] It is recommended that all electronic incoming and outgoing mail pass through the general space and that all non-electronic incoming and outgoing mail pass through the records office. However, it is also recommended that the electronic incoming mail which contains the specific address of the individual space proceed directly to it after receiving a registration number.

[8] A record profile is one of the manifestations of the conceptual action of setting aside a document, an action which gives rise to the archival bond and which transforms the document into a record. For the definitions of set aside and archival bond, see glossary

[9] It is recommended that, every time the order to send or close an electronic record or to consign a non-electronic record to the central record system is given, a record profile form be generated. For electronic records, as many of the fields of the record profile as possible will be filled by the system. The system will prompt the office/officer to fill in the remaining fields on the form, depending on the space in which the office/officer is operating.

[10] It is recommended that all non-electronic records which must be consigned to the central records system and/or transmitted to the outside be sent to the records office, which creates for each record a record profile in the general space of the electronic system, registers it and consigns it to the central records system. In the case of incoming and internal records, the original is consigned to the central records system. In the case of outgoing records, a copy, containing the registry number and classification code, is consigned to the central records system.

[11] The fact that all the fields must be included on the form does not mean that every field must be filled in for every record made or received. Only the profiles of the records for which maximum reliability and authenticity are required would have all the fields filled in. The records office should be given the authority to designate specific fields as optional depending upon the status and mode of transmission of the record, legal requirements, or other relevant factors. Such designation should be electronically enforced so that each officer will be prompted to fill in only those fields required.

[12] The protocol number is the consecutive number assigned to each incoming or outgoing record in the protocol register. With non-electronic records, the protocol number must be copied as a management annotation onto the record.

[13] Date of receipt is the date the record is received by the agency to which it was sent. For both electronic and non-electronic records, it corresponds to the date on which the record is assigned a protocol number.

[14] Time of receipt is the time the record is received by the agency to which it was sent. This element is not relevant to non-electronic records, except in very specific circumstances regulated by legal requirements.

[15] Date of transmission is the date the record leaves the space in which it was generated, either to go from one space to another or from the general space to outside the agency or from the records office to outside the agency.

[16] Time of transmission is the time the record leaves the space in which it generated. This element is not relevant to non-electronic records, except in very specific circumstances regulated by legal requirements.

[17] The date of a record corresponds to the date assigned to it by the author. It appears in the intellectual form of the record, specifically in the content articulation.

[18] The archival date of a record is the date assigned to it by the record office. For electronic records, the archival date is the date a record is received into the general space of the electronic system. For non-electronic records, the archival date is the date that appears on the date stamp affixed to the record by the records office.

[19] The protocol number of sending office is the protocol number assigned to the record by the agency sending it. This element is only relevant in cases where the sending agency uses a protocol register to control its incoming and outgoing records.

[20] The originator's name is the name of the person from whose electronic address the record has been sent. See First Progress Report, p. 225.

[21] The originator's address is the electronic address from which the record has been sent.

[22] The author's name is the name of the person competent to issue the record or in whose name or by whose command the record has been issued. See Luciana Duranti, "Diplomatics: New Uses for an Old Science (Part III)," Archivaria 30 (Summer 1990), pp. 5-14.

[23] The author's address is the address of the person competent to issue the record or in whose name or by whose command the record has been issued.

[24] The writer's name is the name of the person competent for the articulation of the content of the record. See Luciana Duranti, "Diplomatics: New Uses for an Old Science (Part III)," Archivaria 30 (Summer 1990), pp. 5-14.

[25] The writer's address is the address of the person competent for the articulation of the content of the record.

[26] Action or matter is the fact that triggers the issuing of the record. See Luciana Duranti, "Diplomatics: New Uses for an Old Science (Part II)," Archivaria 29 (Winter 1989-90), pp. 5-16.

[27] Number of attachments is the number of previously autonomous items that have been linked inextricably to the record before transmission in order for it to accomplish its purpose.

[28] See glossary

[29] The handling office is the office competent for treating a matter.

[30] Action taken, in the case in which the record described in the profile does not require a written response, is the specific non-written act taken in response to the receipt of the record. For example, if the action taken in response to receiving a record is to make a phone call, that action would be recorded in the Action taken field of the protocol register. Similarly, if the only action taken in response to receiving a record is consigning it to the central records system for reference purposes, the action of consigning it to the central records system would be recorded in the Action taken field of the protocol register.

[31] The addressee's name is the name of the person to whom the record is directed or for whom the record is intended. See Luciana Duranti, "Diplomatics: New Uses for an Old Science (Part III)," Archivaria 30 (Summer 1990), pp. 5-14.

[32] The addressee's address is the address of the person to whom the record is directed or for whom the record is intended.

[33] The receiver's name is the name of each person to whom the record is copied for information purposes.

[34] The receiver's address is the address of each person to whom the record is copied for information purposes.

[35] The class code of the record is that component of the classification code which corresponds to the code of the class in which the record belongs, as it appears in the classification scheme.

[36] The dossier identifier of the record is that component of the classification code which corresponds to the identifier for the dossier in which the record belongs. It may be constituted by the name of a person or organization, a symbol, a progressive number, a date, or a specific topic within the class's general subject.

[37] The record item identifier is that component of the classification code which corresponds to the progressive number of the record within the dossier (or, in the absence of dossiers, within the specific class). This identifier is assigned to the record when it is consigned to the central records system. The record item identifier is the final component of the classification code.

[38] See glossary

[39] Draft number is the consecutive number assigned to sequential drafts of the same record.

[40] When records in the general space are consulted, they are not transmitted to the space in which they are consulted, but viewed from there. Transmission of a record from the general space implies the creation of a copy of the record in the space in which the record is consulted. Such copy is, in fact, a new record and may be modified at will by the person having jurisdiction over the space in which the copy exists.

[41] See (e) above.

[42] It is recommended that the registration data be taken from the record profile fields. In such a case, the fields of the record profile may be distinguished in three categories: fields having an identification purpose (e.g., class code), fields filled for purposes of both identification and registration (e.g., author, addressee), and fields filled only for purpose of registration (e.g., protocol number).

[43] It is recommended that all the fields listed in (i) or (k), as applicable, be included in the protocol register.

[44] It is recommended that a new protocol register be opened at the beginning of either the calendar year or the fiscal year according to the needs of the agency, and that its time span be precisely one year. The first day of each year, the consecutive number would begin with (1) and each register will be identified by the name of the agency, the year it covers, and the inclusive numbers within it.

[45] For definition of status of transmission, see glossary

[46] The original is the first complete and effective document. In order to be an original, a document must present three characteristics: completeness (i.e., its physical form and intellectual form must be

the one intended by its author), primitiveness (i.e., it must be the first to be produced in its complete form) and effectiveness (i.e., it must be capable of reaching the effects for which it was produced).

[47] A draft is a temporary compilation of a document intended for correction. Drafts may be in various stages of completion.

[48] A copy is a reproduction of a record., which may be made from an original record, from a previous copy or, from a draft.

[49] In an electronic system any record that has not been transmitted is considered a draft because the act of transmitting it across electronic boundaries necessarily adds components to the record which make it complete.

[50] Description refers to an abbreviated version of the record profile which includes only the action or matter and the archival and record dates.

[51] Subject files are an example of ongoing dossiers that are routinely closed annually and then reopened for the next year. The dossier name and code is identical for all these files, but each one refers to one year. Student files or other types of case files, on the other hand, are examples of dossiers that remain open until the matter to which they refer is concluded.

[52] If the class does not contain dossiers, create a final view of all the record profiles of all the records for each year before removing them from the system. The creation of a final view is a way of freezing the relationships among the records and thus serves the purpose of authenticating them.

[53] It is recommended that location information for these records be controlled by the records office.

[54] It is recommended that the agency use, as a basis for thesaurus construction, the appropriate standard, e.g., ANSI/NISO Z39.19-1993 (Guidelines for the Construction, Format and Management of Monolingual Thesauri), ISO 2788-1986 (Guidelines for the Establishment and Development of Monolingual Thesauri), ISO 5964-1985 (Guidelines for the Establishment and Development of Multilingual Thesauri).

[55] The audit trail is designed to fulfill the sole purpose of audit by the agency itself or by external auditors. It is expected that, once the audit is completed, the audit trail is destroyed unless differently prescribed by law.

[56] The specific rules governing auditing procedures are based on work done previously by William E. Underwood, one of the members of the U.S. DoD research team.

[57] Metadata of the electronic system are composed of the data which describe the operating system, the program generating the records, the physical location of the records in the electronic system (data directory) and the value of each data element (data dictionary). In contrast, the metadata of the records are the data which place the record within its documentary and administrative context at the moment of creation, the same data which are assembled into the record profile. For a discussion of the metadata of the records, see Heather MacNeil, "Metadata Strategies and Archival Description: Comparing Apples to Oranges," Archivaria 39 (Spring 1995), pp. 22-32.

[58] The reason for determining, for each procedure, what type it is, is to assess which procedures require the most control to ensure that the office/officers will be fully accountable for their actions. Because constitutive procedures are the ones through which the agency creates, extinguishes, or modifies the situation of persons with whom it interacts, they require the most control aimed to guaranteeing the reliability and authenticity of the records they produce. On the other hand, instrumental procedures, which do not directly result in any action, are the most effective when they are the least controlled.

[59] Constitutive procedures are those procedures which create, extinguish or modify the exercise of power of the addressee. Constitutive procedures may be categorized as procedures of concession, of limitation, or of authorization, and their purpose is to fulfill the agency's mandate.

[60] Executive procedures are those procedures which allow for the regular transaction of affairs according to rules established by a different authority, e.g., personnel, finances.

[61] Instrumental procedures are those procedures which are connected to the expression of opinions and advice.

[62] Organizational procedures are those procedures, the purpose of which is to establish organizational structure and internal procedures and to maintain, modify or extinguish them.

[63] The initiative phase comprises those acts that start the mechanism of the procedure.

[64] The inquiry phase comprises the collection of the elements necessary to evaluate the situation.

[65] The consultation phase comprises the collection of opinions and advice after the relevant information has been assembled.

[66] The deliberation phase is constituted by the decision-making.

[67] The deliberation control phase consists of the control exercised by a person different from those making the decision on the substance and/or form of the deliberation.

[68] The execution phase consists of all the actions that give a formal character to the deliberation, such as the validation, communication, notification, or publication of the related record. For the diplomatic phases of a procedure see Luciana Duranti, "Diplomatics: New Uses for an Old Science (Part IV)," Archivaria 31 (Winter 1990-91), pp. 14-19.

[69] As can be seen in the entity model, a procedure is composed of acts (alias action, see glossary) and each act is identified by a record.

[70] The records are identified, not only on the basis of their intellectual form, but, also, on the basis of their function with respect to the action to which they relate (whether dispositive, probative, supporting, or narrative. For the meaning of these terms, see glossary).

[71] A dispositive record is a record whose written form is required as the essence and substance of the act. A dispositive record is identified with the act itself, therefore it constitutes the strongest evidence of it (The means by which any matter of fact is established or disproved. That which demonstrates, makes clear, or ascertains the truth or existence of a fact).

[72] Make document means to compile a document in its intended form. The compilation includes the various stages of drafting the document as well as the production of the original.

[73] A probative record is a record whose written form is required as proof that an act has taken place. A probative record is evidence of an already completed act.

[74] A supporting record is a record on which an act is based, but whose written form is optional. A supporting record is connected to an act but is not substance or evidence of it.

[75] A narrative record is a record that serves as memory of an act , but whose written form is optional. A narrative record is information about an act, but is not generated as substance or evidence of it.

[76] The act of requesting records leads to retrieved records.

[77] The requirement stipulated here is that agencies must register every incoming electronic document that passes through the general, group and individual spaces. Agencies should develop procedures, therefore, for ensuring that junk mail directed to an agency, such as bulletin board, listserv, commercial, teleconferencing and similar types of messages, is sent directly to the private e-mail address of the individuals within the agency who are subscribers rather than going to the individual space or, if the agency is the subscriber, to a specific address dedicated to that purpose (i.e., a junk mail space), to avoid having it enter the agency's general space and be registered as records. As for non-electronic junk mail, anything which is preprinted should be sent to the agency's library or resource centre (if one exists) or destroyed, without a protocol number or record profile being attached to it.

[78] A repertory of dossiers is created for each lowest hierarchical subdivision (class) of each primary class within the classification scheme. It identifies all the dossiers that have been opened within each of these lowest classes in the order prescribed in the scope note of the class itself within the classification scheme. The entry for each dossier in the repertory includes the name of the dossier, the names of its subdossiers (if applicable), and its routing through administrative offices during its life cycle.

[79] It is recommended that an electronic repertory of dossiers be established to permit the immediate recording of a new dossier when it is opened.

[80] Examples of the rules necessary for creating a register entry are as follows:
a) when an incoming record is received, create a register entry in which:
1.   protocol number is the next sequential number in the protocol register for the year;
2.   if the record is the first of the first day of the year, the numerical sequence starts again
3.   date of receipt is assigned value of record profile's date of receipt;
4.   date of transmission is assigned value of record profiles date of transmission;
5.   time of transmission is assigned value of record profile's time of transmission taken from the header of the electronic mail message. Time of transmission is not assigned a value for non-electronic record;
6.   date of record is assigned value of record's date;

7.   the protocol number of sending office is that appearing on the incoming record profile;
8.   if the record is e-mail, the originator's name is assigned value of the prefix of the e-mail address in the originator's name field of the register entry;
9.   if the record is non-electronic, value is not assigned to the originator's name field;
10. if the record is e-mail, the originator's address is entered in the originator's address field of the entry;
11. if the record is non-electronic, value is not assigned to the originator's address field;
12. if the record is e-mail, and the author is different from the originator, the author's name is entered in the author's name field of the register entry;
13. if the record is e-mail, and the author is the same as the originator, the originator's name is entered in the author's name field of the register entry;
14. if the record is non-electronic, the author's name is entered in the author's name field;
15. if the record is e-mail, and the author is different from the originator, the author's address is entered in the author's address field of the register entry;
16. if the record is e-mail, and the author is the same as the originator, the originator's address is entered in the author's address field of the register entry;
17. if the record is non-electronic, the author's address is entered in the author's address field.
18. the action or matter to which the record pertains is entered in the action or matter field of the entry;
19. if the record is non-electronic, and it has attachments, enter the number of attachments in the attachment field of the register entry;
20. the medium of the record is entered in the medium field;
21. the mode of transmission, e.g. post, e-mail, fax, courier, is entered in the mode of transmission field of the register entry;

b) If a record is outgoing, then create a register entry in which:
1.   the next consecutive integer to the protocol number is automatically assigned;
2.   the date the record is transmitted is entered in the date of transmission field;
3.   if the record is e-mail, the time of transmission of the record is entered in the time of transmission field;
4.   the date of the record is entered in the date of the record field;
5.   the action or matter of the record is entered ...;
6.   the number of attachments is entered...;
7.   the medium of the record is entered...;
8.   the addressee's name is entered...;
9.   the addressee's address is entered...;
10. the class code and dossier identifier (if applicable) is entered...
11. the mode of transmission is entered...;

[81] The record item identifier is that component of the classification code which corresponds to the progressive number of the record within the dossier (or, in the absence of dossiers, within the specific class). One way to assign the number would be to design a system that automatically assigns a record item identifier to the record profile of each electronic and non-electronic record when that record is consigned to the central records system.

[82] The archival date of a record is the date assigned to it by the records office. For electronic records, the archival date is the date a record is received into the general space of the electronic system. For non-electronic records, it is the date that appears on the date stamp affixed to the record by the records office.

[83] Because records that are consigned to the central records system cannot be modified, only views of electronic records are retrieved.

[84] A simple copy is the mere transcription of the content of the original.

[85] An imitative copy reproduces, either completely or partially, the content and form of the original record.

[86] An authentic copy is a copy certified by authorized officials so as to render it legally admissible as evidence.

[87] For electronic records, removal from the central records system implies that the removed records cannot be retrieved by any means from that system.

[88] The records' registration entries in the protocol register will remain in the system for as long as the retention period for the protocol register requires.

Appendix E
Entity Model

INTRODUCTION

The entity model has been developed using a standard modeling technique that consists of the steps described below.

1. definition of the "entities", that is, sets of real or abstract things, involved with the highest level activity and all its component activities. Each entity must be made up of things having common attributes or characteristics, must have a unique name with always the same meaning, and can have any number of relationships with the other entities identified.
2. definition of the specific and non-specific relationships which associate the identified entities, and their representation by means of connecting lines ending with symbols such as a diamond, meaning "0 or 1", a bullet, meaning "1 or many", or a circle, meaning "instance of";
3. definition of the attributes of each entity. "Attributes" are the characteristics or properties associated with each entity, whereas "attribute instances" are specific characteristics of individual members of the entity.[1]

An entity model, built according to IDEF language, cannot include entities for which there is not more than one instance. Entities representing archival concepts of which there is only one instance (i.e., agency, classification scheme, recordkeeping system, competent archival body), therefore, appear on the model as context entities and they are shown at the top of the model above the solid black horizontal line, along with their identifying relationships. For example, "an agency has one recordkeeping system," "a recordkeeping system includes one classification scheme," and "one recordkeeping system includes one protocol register per year."

Following the entity model image is a list of list of attributes of record and dossier. All terms shown on the entity model are defined in the glossary.

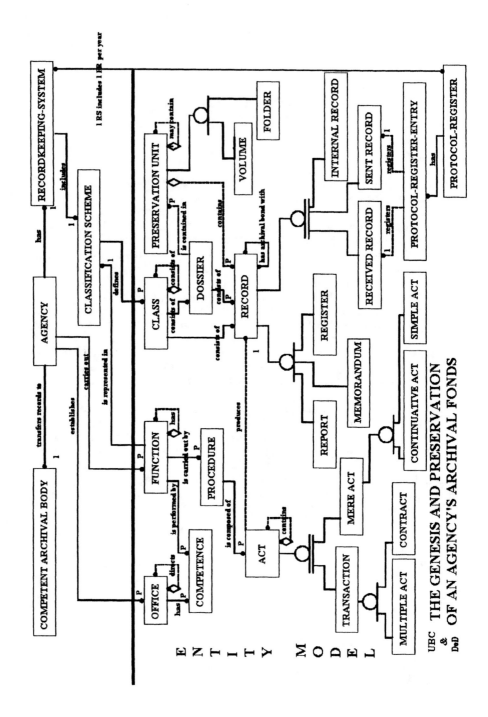

UBC　THE GENESIS AND PRESERVATION
&
DoD　OF AN AGENCY'S ARCHIVAL FONDS

ATTRIBUTES OF ENTITIES DEPICTED ON ENTITY MODEL

Attributes are the characteristics or properties associated with each entity. Attributes have been defined for the entities "record" and "dossier".

In metadata development, entity attributes are transformed into codes.

1. Attributes of RECORD
1.1 Attributes of GENERIC RECORD. The attributes listed below apply to records of all types.

- Record item identifier (the component of the classification code which corresponds to the progressive number of the record within the dossier or, in the absence of dossiers, within the specific class)

- Dossier identifier (the component of the classification code which corresponds to the identifier for the dossier in which the record belongs. It may be constituted by the name of a person or organization, a symbol, a progressive number, a date, or a specific topic within the class's general subject)

- Class code (the component of the classification code which corresponds to the code of the class in which the record belongs, as it appears in the classification scheme)

- Author's name (the name of the person competent to issue the record or in whose name or by whose command the record has been issued)

- Author's address (the address of the person competent to issue the record or in whose name or by whose command the record has been issued)

- Writer's name (the name of the person competent for the articulation of the content of the record)

- Writer's address (the address of the person competent for the articulation of the content of the record)

- Addressee's name (the name of the person to whom the record is directed or for whom the record is intended)

- Addressee's address (the address of the person to whom the record is directed or for whom the record is intended)

- Medium (the physical carrier upon which the record is recorded or stored)

- Record date (the date assigned to a record by its author)

- Date of transmission (the date the record leaves the space in which it was generated, either to go from one space to another or from the general space to outside the agency or from the records office to outside the agency)

- Archival date (the date assigned to a record by the record office at the time it assigns the record item identifier)

- Action or matter (the fact that triggers the issuing of the record)

- Handling office (the office competent for treating a matter)

- Security classification (the level of protection assigned to a record)

- Mode of transmission (the manner in which a record is dispatched, e.g., post, e-mail, fax, courier)

- Status of transmission (the state of a record when it is initially made or received and set aside. The state may be draft, original, or copy)

- Physical form (the formal attributes of the record that determine its external makeup. It includes script (e.g., type font, format, inserts, colours, etc.), language, special signs, seals (including digital signatures, time-stamps, etc.). For electronic records it includes those parts of the technological context that determine what the record will look like and how it will be accessed, e.g., the configuration and architecture of the electronic operating system, the architecture of electronic records, the software)

- Intellectual form--content configuration (the type of representation of the content, whether text, graphic, image, sound, or a combination thereof)

- Intellectual form--content articulation (the elements of the discourse and their arrangement, e.g., date, salutation, exposition, disposition, etc.)

- Intellectual form--annotations (additions made to the record after its creation, such as the record profile, the date-stamp, the endorsement, the bring forward symbol)

1.2 Attributes of CATEGORY RECORD. The attributes listed below apply to only certain types of records. For example, the attribute "protocol number" applies only to incoming and outgoing records.

- Protocol number (the consecutive number assigned to each incoming or outgoing record in the protocol register. With non-electronic records, the protocol number must be copied as a management annotation onto the record)

- Date of receipt (date the record is received by the agency to which it was sent. For both electronic and non-electronic records, it corresponds to the date on which the record is assigned a protocol number)

- Time of receipt (the time the record is received by the agency to which it was sent. This element is not relevant to non-electronic records except in very specific circumstances regulated by legal requirements)

- Time of transmission (the time the record leaves the space in which it generated. This element is not relevant to non-electronic records, except in very specific circumstances regulated by legal requirements)

- Protocol number of sending office (the protocol number assigned to the record by the agency sending it. This element is only relevant in cases where the sending agency uses a protocol register to control its incoming and outgoing records)

- Originator's name (the name of the person from whose electronic address the record has been sent)

- Originator's address (the electronic address from which the record has been sent)

- Number of attachments (the number of previously autonomous items that have been linked inextricably to the record before transmission in order for it to accomplish its purpose)

- Receiver's name (the name of each person to whom the record is copied for information purposes)

- Receiver's address (the address of each person to whom the record is copied for information purposes)

- Draft number (the consecutive number assigned to sequential drafts of the same record)

2. Attributes of DOSSIER
2.1 Attributes of GENERIC DOSSIER. The attributes listed below apply to dossiers of all types.

- Dossier identifier (the component of the classification code which corresponds to the identifier for the dossier. It may be constituted by the name of a person or organization, a symbol, a progressive number, a date, or a specific topic within the class's general subject)

- Class code (the component of the classification code which corresponds to the code of the class in which the record belongs, as it appears in the classification scheme)

- Dossier open date (the date a dossier is created)

- Dossier close date (the date that a dossier is closed)

2.2 Attributes of CATEGORY DOSSIER. Attributes have not been defined for category dossiers.

Appendix F
List Of Articles Relating To The Research

1. Duranti, Luciana and Heather MacNeil. "The Protection of the Integrity of Electronic Records: An Overview of the UBC-MAS Research Project." *Archivaria* 42 (Fall 1996): 46-67.
2. Duranti, Luciana. "Reliability and Authenticity: The Concepts and their Implications." *Archivaria* 39 (Spring 1995): 5-10.
3. Duranti, Luciana and Heather MacNeil. "Protecting Electronic Evidence: A Third Progress Report on a Research Study and its Methodology." *Archivi & Computer* anno VI, fasc. 5 (1996): 343-404.
4. Duranti, Luciana, Heather MacNeil and William E. Underwood, "Protecting Electronic Evidence: A Second Progress Report on a Research Study and its Methodology." *Archivi & Computer* anno VI, fasc. 1 (1996): 37-70.
5. Duranti, Luciana and Terry Eastwood. "Protecting Electronic Evidence: A Progress Report on a Research Study and its Methodology." *Archivi & Computer* anno V: fasc. 3 (1995):213-250.
6. Eastwood, Terry. "Reliable and Authentic Electronic Records." In *Proceedings of the 1996 Annual Meeting of the American Society of Information Science*. Silver Springs, MD: American Society of Information Science, 1996.
7. MacNeil, Heather. "Protecting Electronic Evidence: A Final Progress Report on a Research Study and Its Methodology." *Archivi & Computer* anno VII, fasc. 1 (1997): 22-35.
8. MacNeil, Heather. "The Implications of the UBC Research Results for Archival Description in General and the Canadian Rules for Archival Description in Particular." *Archivi & Computer* anno VI, fasc. 2 (1996): 239-46.
9. Thibodeau, Kenneth and Daryll R. Prescott. "Reengineering Records Management: The U.S. Department of Defense, Records Management Task Force." *Archivi & Computer* anno VI, fasc. 1 (1996): 71-78.

Index

See also Actions; Components
    of records; Form; Persons;
    Procedures
housekeeping. *See* Administrative
    records
identification of, 3-4
integrity of. *See* Integrity
domains. *See* Records
    management domains
    See also General space; Group
        space; Individual space
migration of, 13
office. *See* Records office
procedures for keeping. *See*
    Procedures
profile. *See* Record profile
program. *See* Operational records
registration of. *See* Registration
reliability of. *See* Reliability;
    Reliable records
reliable records. *See* Reliability;
    Reliable records
reproduction of, 13
retention of. *See* Retention of
    records
    See also Disposition; Retention
        schedule
retrieval of. *See* Retrieval of
    records
tracking and locating of, 50
traditional. *See* Traditional
    environment; Traditional
    records
transfer of. *See* Transfer of
    records
trustworthiness of, 4, 25
Records management, 55-57
Records management domains, 40-
    41
    See also General space; Group
        space; Individual space
Records office, 33, 35, 41-42, 50-55
Records preservation system, 39
    See also Central records
        system; Recordkeeping
        system; Records system
Records schedule, 52-53
Records system, 39

See also Central records
    system; Recordkeeping
    system; Records
    preservation system
Register, 48-49
    See also Protocol register;
        Registration
Registration, 48-49
    See also Classification; Record
        profile; Register
Reliability, 5-6, 23, 25-27, 32, 39,
    41-43, 49
    See also Authenticity;
        Completeness; Integrity;
        Reliable records
Reliable records, 27, 39
    See also Reliability; Authentic
        records
Repertory of dossiers, 36
    See also Dossiers; Dossier
        identifier
Reproduction of records. *See*
    Records, reproduction of
Retention of records, 52-53
    See also Disposition; Integrated
        classification scheme and
        retention schedule;
        Retention schedule
Retention schedule, 52-53
    See also Disposition; Integrated
        classification scheme and
        retention schedule;
        Retention of records
Retrieval of records, 35-37, 50

Semi-active records, 54-55
    See also Active records;
        Inactive records
State of transmission. *See*
    Transmission
Subject files, 47
Supporting records, 18
    See also Dispositive records;
        Narrative records; Probative
        records

Technological context. *See* Context
Technological obsolescence, 40

Printed in the United States
951500001B